WE'RE NOT MONSTERS

Teens Speak Out about Teens in Trouble

Sabrina Solin Weill

Harper
tempest

An Imprint of HarperCollins*Publishers*

Library of Congress Cataloging-in-Publication Data
Weill, Sabrina Solin.
  We're not monsters : teens speak out about teens in trouble / Sabrina Solin
Weill.
      p.   cm.
  ISBN 0-380-80703-3 (pbk.) — ISBN 0-06-029543-0 (lib. bdg.)
  1. Juvenile delinquents—United States—Juvenile literature.
2. Teenagers—United States—Interviews—Juvenile literature.
3. Adolescent psychology—Juvenile literature.   [1. Juvenile delinquency.]
I. Title.
HV9104.W435   2001   2001024619
364.36'0973—dc21   CIP
                                                                         AC

Typography by Henrietta Stern
❖
First HarperTempest edition, 2002

Visit us on the World Wide Web!
www.harperteen.com

There are people whose contributions to this book were invaluable. Thanks, first of all, to my editor Ruth Katcher. Thanks also to Laura Gilbert, Sadie Van Gelder, Atoosa Rubenstein, Rachel Aydt, Tommy Dunne, Francesca Rea, Ann Shoket, and Scot Bontrager. Thanks to my family, both the Solins and the Weills, for your constant suport while I worked on this project.

To all the teenagers who shared their lives, thank you for being so open, so honest, and willing to tell your stories to show other teens that they're not alone.

Visit *www.werenotmonsters.com* to talk about the issues in this book or tell your story.

For Steven
who taught me about perspective

Contents

"The media does not portray teens in the proper light. It is one extreme or the other. We are either viewed as drug-abusing, alcoholic, suicidal rebels or as hormone-driven airheads who don't know the difference between reality and fiction. Teens are, for the most part, somewhere in the middle. We have fun, we laugh at stupid things, we giggle when someone we like likes us back, and we also go through tough stuff. I know because I have had friends die from suicide, from overdoses, or in car crashes. We do some bad stuff sometimes, stuff we know we shouldn't but we do, just because. I've known people who have been abused and people who are the abusers, and that's all real to a teen. I've been in love—not 'puppy love' but real love. And it angers me when all of this, our lives, are made light of and turned into an afternoon-special cliché. Not every teen experiences all of this, but whatever they experience is real, and it shouldn't be pushed aside with a quick 'You're too young to know what it's really like.' That's probably the most important thing to me: to know that people see that teens are real, not some cheesy portrayal on TV."

—Susie, 15

Introduction

IF YOU WATCH THE NEWS or read the papers, or listen to the whispers in the halls of any high school, you know that each day greets us with more bad news about teenagers. Teens are shooting each other, molesting younger kids, banding in gangs and terrorizing inner cities and bucolic towns. They are driving drunk, beating their girlfriends, and having unprotected sex at an alarming rate. Girls are maturing sooner and getting pregnant younger—and in many cases, the father is over twenty-one years old. Teenage girls are hiding their pregnancies and stashing their infants in a girls' room at the prom, in Dumpsters, or under hotel beds to be found by horrified janitors. What's most scary of all, some would argue, is that they're acting just like adults.

Every time one of the more outrageous teen-perpetrated incidents gets reported to the media, the experts tell us to turn off the TV or keep minors out of the latest movie, because those images are teaching kids how to set subway clerks on fire. And by all means, keep them off the Internet, which is giving out bomb-making instructions alongside recipes for famous-brand chocolate chip cookies.

It might be true that the media is turning teens against

the world and against each other. There are enough books on the topic and experts who support the theory. Other experts who study teenagers say disintegration of the family is to blame. Kids aren't getting enough attention at home, so they're acting out or joining gangs in an effort to claim the family they so desperately want. It's biological, say still other experts, citing brain studies of incarcerated teens.

But no matter how many studies are done or how many explanations experts offer, the question doesn't seem to go away: Why are teens acting this way? Is there something we can point to, some change we can see, or something they have learned that's making them go haywire? And more importantly, what can we do to recognize kids in trouble and get them help before they go astray? Before they become a statistic, a headline, like Andrew Golden and Mitchell Johnson?

On March 24, 1998, Andrew Golden, age eleven, pulled the fire alarm at his Jonesboro, Arkansas, middle school and ran to the nearby woods where Mitchell Johnson, 13, was hiding with enough gunpower and ammunition to kill hundreds of people. Moments later, the two shot at students and teachers as they filed outside. Four female students and one female teacher were killed; ten others were wounded.

Minutes after the news broke, the theories started flying: Andrew had gun-crazy parents. Mitchell had a traumatic early childhood. The kids were desensitized to violence, a result of too many hours logged in front of video games and violent movies. But those closest to the incident had a totally different take. Classmates at Westside Middle School created and hung a large sign for Mitchell. It said: WE FORGIVE YOU.

"I sleep with a Bible under my pillow," said Candace Porter, the eleven-year-old who said she broke up with Mitchell days before the shooting. "I knew he was trouble." That was all the *New York Post* could get out of Candace, no doubt after she had been besieged by other members of the press despite her recent gunshot wound. We are left wondering: How did she know Mitchell was bad news? What signs did he show? Why did she think he would do something so dramatic, so wrong? Does she see the same signs in other kids in her class? In herself?

The only way to find out what's going on in teenagers' minds is to ask them: the real, not-famous teenagers who may or may not have encountered extraordinary circumstances. This is what I have done. I have talked with and e-mailed hundreds of teenagers from all walks of life, from one-movie-theater towns and big cities, from wealthy bedroom communities and inner-city projects. Teens who have done wrong and teens who have not. Teens who know too much about pain and ugliness and teens who know of no such thing. If you're a teenager, I talked with you, or your friends, or kids you might hang out with. If you're a parent, I talked to kids like yours.

Finding teenagers to interview was easy—almost everyone I mentioned this project to was eager to contribute his or her voice. From my years as an editor of an educational magazine for teenagers, I know a lot of teachers who kindly passed out questionnaires to kids, giving them the option to be interviewed. I spoke with gang-intervention specialists and directors of homes for teen mothers and intake psychologists at major children's hospitals, all of whom lent me their expertise and their teen contacts. My colleague, journalist Laura Gilbert, conducted dozens of interviews. Web producer Scot Bontrager set up a posting on an Internet site asking teenagers to share their views on these topics, and the response was incredible. Hundreds of teens wrote in, wanting to be heard. I've used only their first names or, in a few cases, left out or changed their names and identifying features, for the sake of their privacy. In all cases, I've edited their stories very little.

In every high school there are secrets and rumors and half-truths to be uncovered. In researching this book, I heard stories of hope, heartbreak, and extraordinary circumstances. A girl from a tiny, quiet Vermont town told me about her high school, which had received more than twenty bomb threats in one year. A Colorado boy talked about being beaten with baseball bats for the pleasure of gaining entry into a gang, where he was coerced, sometimes forcibly, into harming others. A middle-class girl from Georgia told me that sometimes she wished she could die. A pregnant sixteen-year-old talked about decorating her dream house in shades of cranberry.

To the extent that teens who hurt and kill and molest made no sense to me before I embarked on this project, they make more sense now—and I hope this book has the same effect on you. Teens in America are walking a tightrope without a net. Caught between childhood and adulthood, teens are left holding the worst attributes of each world. Some have parents who are too busy for them, others, parents who are horrifyingly abusive—some teens had to be excluded from this collection because their own horrors so far exceeded those I wanted them to comment on.

During the teen years, everything is felt so deeply. Teens become fiercely angry and incredibly distraught at slights that most adults have learned to brush off. The flip side of this is that teens exhibit a passion (for ideas, causes, friends, other people) rarely seen in adults.

But when you add to this temperament a tendency toward impulsiveness, a feeling of immortality, a tenuous-at-best connection to their schools or communities, changing hormones, and an overall feeling of injustice about the way the world has treated you . . . you have one angry person: one who doesn't care what happens to himself or herself; someone who believes that no matter what he or she does, the outcome will be the same. The scary thing is, this is the way a lot of teens feel.

Of course, many young people—the vast majority—are able to overcome these feelings and wait out the crazy hormones and muddle their way through the teen years. In other words, they become adults. But what of the others? The kids who are just a little closer to the edge? They are in every school and every town—sometimes you can walk into school and point them out; other times they blend in so well, you'd never guess what they're really thinking. What keeps most kids from making the transition from offbeat to dangerous? What pushes those unlucky few over the edge? To find out, I talked to the leading experts in the field of teen psychology and psychiatry—and, of course, to tons of teenagers. Here's what they had to say.

" I think adults miss something very important about teenagers. They accuse a kid to his face of 'being the kind of kid that would bring a gun to school' because the person does not follow mainstream philosophy or espouses contempt for those who do.

For instance, my principal does not like the group I'm part of. We appreciate weapons such as swords and katanas, we have imagination, enjoy animé and literature, we attempt to apply logic and balance to our interactions with society. This brings us into conflict with his ideas.

He abuses his authority. He expelled a kid for calling him a Nazi. Now, there are lots of intermediary steps before expulsion, every one of which he skipped in that case. He's in charge because he likes power trips, and so anything or anyone that could threaten him is banished or battered. He was the one who yelled the gun comment straight into my friend's face. And unfortunately, he is only one out of the majority of authority figures who abuse their power without understanding the consequences.

They think teenagers are vicious, dangerous little vortexes of evil and make accordingly unfair rules. They all miss something very important, however, that completely disproves their assumptions. Many 'freaks' and intellectuals, standouts from the crowd, are lacking three things for violent action: time, material resources, and, most significantly, interest.

My friends and I, for example: We all have so much more we'd rather do than waste time gathering guns and ammunition and stuff. Money is better spent on animé or tapes or comic books or medieval stuff or food or art. We don't care enough about other students or the administration to do anything large- or even small-scale negative. We're special that way.

But sometimes other people aren't. They have more time or more provocation and anger. And when adults, out of fear, antagonize anyone who is different, they can stir truly deadly situations and people to life. People who will find the time and resources to be destructive.

My friends and I are not harmful. But inconsiderate treatment can stir to terrible action those who are."

—John, 15

Chapter 1

Fatal Anger:
Killer Teens

Aᴘʀɪʟ 20 ʙᴇɢᴀɴ ᴀꜱ ᴀ ɴᴏʀᴍᴀʟ ᴅᴀʏ at Columbine High School. It was weeks away from graduation. It was the Monday after prom. It was free-cookie day. But April 20 was also a day Dylan Klebold and Eric Harris had been plotting for almost a year. The two self-proclaimed "outsider" teens from Littleton, Colorado, had kept a diary and made five videotapes describing the massacre they had planned for their classmates—particularly the preppies and jocks—at Columbine High. They had made pipe bombs, intending to plant them in various parts of the school. When the bombs went off, the two of them were going to go on a shooting spree. Their goal was to kill two hundred and fifty people. On the day of the massacre, the pipe bombs failed to go off; but Eric and Dylan still opened fire and succeeded in murdering thirteen and injuring some twenty-five more.

Later it came out that weeks before, Eric had threatened a classmate, Brooks Brown, and directed Brooks to his Web site to learn his fate. When Brooks' parents got a look at the racist, murderous comments on Eric's Web site, they alerted the police. Brooks' parents say that the police, who were already investigating Eric and Dylan for breaking into a van, failed to follow up on their complaint. If they had, they might have been alarmed enough to check out Eric's and Dylan's homes, where surely they would have found the hundreds of rounds of ammo and homemade bombs.

By shortly after eleven A.M., Eric and Dylan were standing outside the school, shooting students near a parking lot and trading fire with a school security guard. As they made their way through the cafeteria, halls, and library, where they eventually would take their own lives, students fled, screamed, and barricaded themselves in classrooms. Outside, police and SWAT teams gathered while news helicopters hovered; the nation held its breath as the police, unsure of the killers' location, were forced to wait several hours before entering the school.

Like Eric and Dylan, Michael Carneal was an outsider, but one of a different flavor. Michael was a geek. He knew he was a geek, just like you know where you fit into the social scheme of things. Fourteen-year-old Michael's geekiness was the kind you can see: his puny frame, his thick glasses. He wasn't geek chic like Spike Jonze or geeky-smart like *ER*'s Dr. Green or a funny geek like Screech. He wasn't one of those geeks happy to make friends among his own. And he didn't appear to have a special talent, which is the saving grace of many not-so-popular teens (like the mechanical genius motorhead or the musically gifted burnout). Michael was no young Monet; he wasn't a computer whiz; he didn't have a great throwing arm or a knack for guitar.

He was an easy target; people spread rumors about him, and the school gossip sheet said he was gay. The other kids sneered when he passed by—no one wanted to share his locker or be his lab partner. What if his social toxicity was contagious?

You've met this kind of kid. No matter how clear people make it that he's not welcome, he's still got to try to fit in. Except Michael Carneal decided he was tired of trying. Tired of getting only snickers, insults, and rejection. So on December 1, 1997, Michael brought guns—loaded guns—to his Paducah, Kentucky, high school and showed them off to some kids right before their morning prayer circle. It worked. For a few minutes, he was the center of attention—a badass, a rebel, a guy with access to hard-core weaponry. But eventually, conversation turned away from the guy with the guns. Michael couldn't stand losing the spotlight, not after he'd risked getting expelled or arrested, not after he'd tasted what it's like to not be invisible.

So Michael started phase two of his attention-getting attempt: This one, he must have thought, would keep people talking about him for a long time to come. He put earplugs in his ears, lifted a .22 Ruger to his cheek, and started shooting. And shooting. And shooting. Three girls were dead, and five other students were wounded when Michael stopped shooting, handed the rifle over to another kid, and perhaps began to realize what he'd done. "Kill me," he allegedly begged a football player. "Please kill me."

Hours after the incident, Michael's scrawny face was plastered on CNN Interactive and the early evening news, just like the youthful visages of the kids who had shot up their schools before him: Jeremy Strohmeyer, Luke Woodham, Kip Kinkel. . . . And we were left asking ourselves the same questions: What made Michael snap? Was it the constant teasing? Low self-esteem? Were his parents too liberal . . . or too strict? Was he mentally ill? Who can we blame? Is it us?

What's Going On Here?

It's the rare teenager who commits murder, though it's certainly normal to think about it. Whether you're a geek or a varsity athlete, head of the student council or a metalhead, adolescence is a time of intense feeling. Every kiss is more than just a kiss. *(Will he tell everyone I did that? Will he lie? Will she think we're in a relationship? Will I marry this guy? What if I do it wrong?)* And insults are more deeply felt. *(I'm gonna mess her up if she talks to my crush again! No one will ever go out with me again. I failed that test and I'll probably never get anywhere in life!)* It's not stupidity: All teenagers think that way.

When every day presents new dramas, how does a teenager decide what to do? The instinct of most teens would be to go with what will make them look good, feel cool, and to worry about the long-term effects later, if ever. Psychologists call this magical thinking, and it goes something like this: *It won't happen to me. If I'm in a group, nothing bad will happen. Everyone else is doing it. None of this will matter in ten years. I'll never be thirty.* If this kind of thinking sounds familiar, you're not alone. "Almost all teenagers underestimate consequences to themselves as well as others," says Dr. Stephen Grissom, chief psychologist at Oklahoma's L.E.

Rader Center, an agency that treats the worst juvenile offenders in the state. "They can only see things from their perspective. They find it difficult to understand why someone would do something that's different from what they would do." In other words, it's difficult for most teens to put themselves in someone else's shoes, or to see into the future. It's not even unusual for teenagers to say "I don't think about life after high school" or "I don't worry about life past thirty," because they don't expect to live that long.

Most people have had daydreams of getting back at the people who make us maddest: Maybe we shut them up with a grade-A chew-out; KO the school bully with some Jackie Chan–style kung fu action; or silence the school library with a few rounds from our rifles. We see ourselves at the center of attention, impressing everyone, maybe winding up in the news, utterly powerful. Magical thinking is what stops us from seeing the rest of the scenario: hurt feelings, suspension, a classmate who spends the rest of his life in a wheelchair, the long nights in a flea-ridden prison cell.

Magical thinking isn't always a negative thing; it's also what allows people to be so fabulously passionate about causes, about sports, about their own desires. That's how some teens achieve incredible goals. It's a great feeling to *know* that you will prevail. It's the dark side of magical thinking that's so dangerous: when that feeling of power gets combined with negative, vengeful thoughts and impulses. In times when someone feels angry at other students, the magical thinking goes: *I deserve better than this. Those people will pay for what they did to me. I'll show them how powerful I really am. I'm going to be famous one day.*

For some teenagers, intense feelings of resentment and rage have one guaranteed-to-make-me-feel-better outlet: violence. Whether it's a two-punch schoolyard fight or mowing down a physics class with an Uzi, it's magical thinking that lets some teens see physical retaliation as a realistic and viable option.

Ashley, 17 · Worcester, MA

Ashley was one of the hundreds of teenagers who came to an online forum where teens could talk about the issues addressed in this book.

Yesterday, I almost completely lost control of myself at school. There's this guy in my art class. He's one of those people who just likes to get under people's skin, and I am one of those people who, if you've pissed me off, you're gonna know, and you'll probably feel it for a week or two. I know violence isn't the answer, but okay, let me explain.

This guy, he does stuff just to get on my nerves. I know it. He knows I know it. He does things like get way too intimate, and throws things at me. Like yesterday, he grabbed my posterior and then asked me what bra size I wear. I was just completely shocked for a moment. I mean, I don't go around asking guys how long they are when they're fully extended, right? So what on earth made this guy think he could do that kind of thing to me? I'm no piece of meat! That's what went through my mind. So then I turned around to slap the crap outta him, and he was already across the room. So I said, "You know, I would go over there and beat the living crap outta you, but I have work to do, so you just better stay your ass away from me for a year or two or you're gonna be hurtin'."

Naturally, of course, considering the fact that my art class is half freshmen, they all laughed and made a big deal out of it. To me it was perfectly simple. It was the truth. Of course, since I am short and kind of small-looking (with the exception of my bust), everyone in the class except the few who knew me thought I was full of it. So they egged him on. Not that he needed much egging on. Anyhow . . . he just threw stuff at me and generally annoyed me, until he threw this hard little . . . thing at me. I still don't know what it was. All I know is, it hurt.

So I snapped. I'm still not exactly sure what it was that I did. All I remember is that he ran, and somehow I ended up climbing over an art table (those things are almost as tall as I am!) and just barely missed ripping him limb from limb because a few friends of mine caught my arms.

The teacher didn't write either of us up, but he's a cool teacher, and he was subbing, not to mention a bit old . . . so if he had tried to remove the guy, he'd have gotten hurt. I don't blame the teacher. So he (the teacher) told me not to hurt the guy, because he only had the mind of a boy. With my friends pinning my arms to my sides, I had to agree, but I told him if he tried it again, I'd hurt him . . . regardless. The thing that scares me, though, is that I lost control like I did . . . because I was really going to hurt him. I usually only have the intention to scare people when I do things like that, but I was really going to hurt that guy. I scared some of the other kids in my class. I mean, yeah, some of them are sheep, but . . . anyhow, so today, we had our regular teacher back, and she wrote the guy up and he's gone now, probably for good.

The other kids in my class were afraid to talk to me for a bit, which, while I can certainly understand it, was a salt-in-a-wound kind of feeling, because I kind of scared myself. Anyhow, I talked to a guy I practice sight-singing with after school, and that made me feel a little better. But he said it was like Dr. Jekyll and Mrs. Hyde or something, because it was the first time he had seen anyone quiet like me snap.

That made me think.

Who's Doing This?

Lesley Wolfe, director of the Center for Women Policy Studies in Washington, D.C., thinks a lot of the current school violence is a result of boys feeling angry at girls. "You want to believe that boys who do this are just wackos and not that they're all about women-hating—but they are," she says.

"I'm disturbed that these are boys who are deliberately going to school to kill girls," Wolfe continues. "They feel entitled to because they got jilted or whatever, and no amount of locking them up is going to help that." Wolfe and other women's studies experts cite the fact that most of the schoolyard victims were girls and women, and in several of the cases, the boys admitted that they were aiming for girls who they felt had wronged them.

There are historical and social explanations for the fact that males are more likely to use aggression, among them cultural norms that dictate boys should show anger but girls should not; male-oriented violent sports like boxing and football; a military-infused society in which wars are fought mostly by men. "Boys are more naturally concerned with power," says Michael Schulman, psychologist to the hundreds of teens filtered through the Leake-Watts group homes in Yonkers, New York. "When they fight, they will physically try to overpower each other, and when that's done, it's over. But with girls, the way they compete is to undermine each other's intimacy."

Is it fair to say, as the media has after some schoolyard killings, that white boys are the new killers? Well, it's true that white boys are more likely to be school shooters. While 36 percent of murderers in general are white, a *New York Times* survey found that 71 percent of rampage killers (those who murder more than one person in a public setting, like the school shooters) are white. And the majority of teens arrested for murder are male. But girls are getting in on the act, too. Between 1992 and 1996, the number of girls arrested for violent crimes increased by 25 percent, while the levels stayed the same for boys.

Gary, 17 · Pittsfield, MA

Gary is a tall, lanky seventeen-year-old with black hair and huge black eyes. He's full of nervous energy and gestures with his hands when he talks—short, fluttering movements, like a bird inside a too-small

***cage. He lives about three hours outside Boston in a
small town that's been pretty depressed since the
G.E. plant closed down in the 1980s.***

I've actually had some very personal experiences
with violence. I used to be very violent. In seventh
and eighth grade I'd get in fights all the time. In
eighth grade I got beat up every single day on the bus
to school. There was this bully, and I'd have to sit with
him because there was no other seat on the bus. Right
after I'd sit down, wham, bam—he'd start punching
me on the arm and leg repeatedly. He would take his
two fingers and go "Da! Da! Da!" on my chest [slams
his fingers on the table with each "Da!"]. I used to
have bruises on my chest from this—it hurt! Still, it
was just under the level of seriousness so adults didn't
pay attention to the problem. A black eye would be
different—people would have told him to stop then.

It was horrible, and there was no way out of it. I
was way into Christianity at the time, and I was like,
"Okay, this is my time of suffering." It just sort of
resolved when we graduated from eighth grade and I
went to high school. I've changed so much since then
through the fact that my father moved out of the
house. I also have a lot of influences: teachers and
ministers who helped me.

My dad was a violent guy. He kept things tense;
you know what I mean? It was a big release of tension
when he left. Recently, I've gotten progressively more
violent for some reason, and without my drama class,
I don't know what would happen. I go in that class and

we do a bunch of mad scenes and I completely lose control. I haven't played sports in a while; maybe I need a release of physical energy. Maybe that's why I'm being more violent.

I have my own gun. I mean, I don't have a personal gun—I use my father's. I have a hunter's permit. Do I feel a sense of satisfaction with a gun in my hand? Not really. It's been a long time since I've shot a gun.

But I understand where those kids accused of shootings are coming from. They just went too far. It's a process of daring yourself. I remember one day I punched a hole in the wall and then I looked over and saw a carpenter's level, and I just dared myself, like "Let's do it." I grabbed the level and I just started slamming things around the house and pounding the door. I beat the door right down. It was crazy. I called my mother, and when she came in and saw what I'd done she just said, "Oh my God" and started crying.

It's such a "live for today" kind of environment now. For adults, time moves slower. But for us, in the heat of anger, there are ways—count-to-ten methods—but that's not safe enough. You can't rely on that. So the thoughts are always there in your head.

I'm still trying to figure out what's going on in the heads of other people, to jump behind their steering wheel. It's terrible to say, but I could be a soldier; I could go out there and kill people for sure. I could rape someone. I have the capacity for it. I have a lot of access to the darker thoughts. I don't think I'm the only one to ever have a thought like that. A lot of people can play it cool and say, "I don't have thoughts like that." They're lying, I think.

I've always been on the outside of all groups, kind of on the outside looking in. I find that a lot of groups are born out of hate; they're kids who are bonding together because of a shared hatred of another kind of kid, know what I mean?

My high school is laced with superficiality. Maybe this is true for every school. I've been going to a homogenous high school. I swear I think they don't let black people into this town. It's like they have a border patrol for black people [he imitates a cop voice]: "Just drive on through and don't look anywhere but straight ahead."

I hope college is different, more diverse. I'm looking at big schools even though I'm a small-town guy. I have a specific major—music theory and composition—so I'm going to have to go to either a conservatory or a big school, and I don't want to go to a conservatory. I want to keep my options open.

Despite the recent news attention on teen killers in middle-class neighborhoods, there are many areas in which teen violence has been the norm for years. "Violence is just a normal thing at school for me," writes an eighteen-year-old girl on a message board. "It happens at least once a week. There was a shooting at my high school. We spent half the day sitting on the floor because the shooters had run through our playground. Luckily, only one person was shot, in the arm, but it could have been much worse. At this high school, violence is pretty common. I remember one week last year when there was a different fight four days in a row."

"People where I live don't last long when they try to act 'hard-core,'" says a fifteen-year-old guy. "People are always trying to compete in my neighborhood, which makes it hard for someone my age to walk around peacefully. At one point, I was robbed. Everything would be more peaceful and safe for my grandparents and me if all these evil people were to go away or stop the violence. You cannot believe how sick and tired I am of walking up my block at night in fear.

"I could not care less about these school shootings. Let's use the Columbine shooting as an example. The two killers were literally outcasts in the social society that is the most important to every teenager: high school. The peer pressure put onto them was extreme—yet they were too weak to overcome it and to ignore the other kids making fun of them. Sure, I am a victim of self-isolation due to many pressures put onto me by others, but I don't use violence to solve my problems."

Why Now?

There are clear statistics showing that boys from violent homes are more likely to become violent, and boys who grow up in violent communities tend to be more violent than boys from safe, rural areas. As for why upper-middle-class boys who have no history of violence at home are becoming increasingly and more intensely violent, there are several theories, each of which has some merit and some flaws.

Is it the media's fault? Look at this situation: In the video store, it's almost nine P.M. In walks a woman with two boys, aged about eight and four. It's clear she's their nanny, not their mom. The eight-year-old picks up a copy of *Halloween H20*, a horror movie, and waves the video box at his caregiver. The younger kid takes his hand out of his mouth and says, "I want to watch it too." The nanny pauses for a minute. "Okay," she says. "But I'm not staying up with you if you have nightmares."

Diane Schetkey, Ph.D., one of the forensic psychologists who examined Michael Carneal, says that for many American boys, their first sexually exciting experience is linked to violent images—much like the ones in the slasher film this eight-year-old is about to stash in his Pokemon backpack. Some studies say watching violent shows (or music videos, or video games) desensitizes kids to violence. The theory goes that as viewers, we get desensitized to yet excited by the violence, so it takes more and more to shock us—or entertain us. We see violence on TV with no punishment, harm, or lasting consequences, and, if nothing in our real life experience counters those images, we may be more likely to use violence in real life. So is the nanny just using harmless bad judgment—or is she helping to shape young potential criminals?

Of course, we all know the difference between something on TV and something in real life, right? Psychologist Martin Glasser, who has been an expert witness for teens accused of murder, points out that most kids can tell the difference between a TV show and real life. "But mentally ill children are affected by these songs and images and do react to them." Glasser tells the story of a sixteen-year-old who thought Marilyn Manson was instructing him to harm people. "Mentally disturbed people fuse themselves with the movie or the song and believe they are part of the song, or the song is directing them to do things." Then again, notorious serial killer Son of Sam thought a dog instructed him to kill, and no one's blaming Fido for violent teenagers. But the frequency and intensity of violence in the media can be provocative to those teenagers who do not have good judgment or a solid sense of self to begin with.

And there are the video games. In the old days, games such as Pong, with its line-and-dot approximation of a Ping-Pong game, didn't inspire violent fantasies the way today's shoot-'em-up, gain-points-for-killing-innocent-bystanders games might. The issue of video games came up in the case of Mitchell Johnson and Andrew Golden, the Arkansas boys who pulled a fire alarm in their school and shot students and teachers as they fled into the courtyard, killing five and wounding ten. It's been well publicized that Golden, eleven at the time of the incident, had used guns before. In the hunting community in which he lived, it was not unusual for kids as young as six to get rifles from Santa, as Golden did. Thirteen-year-old Mitchell Johnson had never held a gun before the incident, yet he proved a remarkably good shot. "In essence," says Schetkey, "kids are training for violence using video games."

Teens can be passionate on the subject of violence. "I go to school in a neighborhood with a trailer park on one side, a bunch of crack shacks on the other, and hookers across the street," wrote one seventeen-year-old girl. "I've seen fights, one where a guy beat his girlfriend with a tennis racket, one where someone beat a 'geek' unconscious with his bike seat, one where twenty guys beat someone up because of a simple racial slur. It always seemed to me, if you are violent, then that's what you use in your life. And this notion that TV, music, and video games encourage it is preposterous. Teens aren't mindless slugs who suck up all the things they see and immediately think, 'Well, if Subzero shot that guy's head off, then I can too!' I mean, it really is moronic. School shootings like the one in Columbine are the result of poor communication, ignorance, low self-esteem, and the ability to get their hands on firearms."

So, are some kids just born bad? The nature vs. nurture question has been raging for centuries. Some people think it's possible for kids to be bad seeds, claiming that such kids are naturally drawn to violent games and movies. Others argue that kids are born with a neutral feeling about violence and are shaped by their environment. Any psychologist will tell you that a kid who is constantly exposed to violence is more likely than other kids to become violent. It makes sense: What you live with, day in and day out, becomes your norm. So if you live with a dad who's constantly beating up your mom (or vice versa), you'll be more likely to beat up your husband or wife in the future. These cycles of abuse are hard to break. But what about kids who live in homes that aren't violent—kids like Kip Kinkel, who grew up in a typical small town in Oregon with caring, law-abiding parents?

What drove Kip to help his mom carry in the groceries one afternoon, then shoot her in the chest? To then shoot his dad in the back of the head? To stay overnight in a house with his two dead parents, then go to school the next day and open fire in the school cafeteria, killing two people and injuring twenty-four? Was he just born bad, or did something happen to make him act the way he did?

"There's always something," says Dr. Stephen Grissom, the chief psychologist at Oklahoma's L.E. Rader Center. He tells the story of a kid at Rader who stabbed another boy to death after that boy and some friends took his cigarette lighter. "So did he kill over the lighter," Grissom asks, "or do we have a kid who has a ton of built-up anger and hostility, and there's a specific combination of events and *bam!*—somebody's dead?"

A *New York Times* study of rampage killers found that the mass murderers involved in school shootings are much more likely to be mentally ill than other teens or adults who murder; they are also more likely to share their plans with their peers and to be prodded on by them. But Grissom's point is that not all kids who kill intend to kill. Some of them just have a burning rage inside them, and they lash out, perhaps without really understanding the full extent of their own power. "Sometimes," Grissom continues, "the difference between a kid who commits murder and a kid who doesn't is the luck of the blow."

Many teenagers seem to understand this delicate balance. "There are times when I'm filled with such rage that everyone takes a step back," writes one sixteen-year-old guy. "There is just so much emotion in me that I forget anything and everything else. Like I can feel no pain and I'll lash out at anybody. Once I made a guy deaf in one ear for a week when I was mad and he teased me. I grabbed his ear, twisted it, and jerked his head down to my knees. I'm shocked at myself afterward. All the violence has come from my family. All my life, my brother has been a trouble-maker. My dad used to beat him with a belt, while I'd be in the next room. Because of this—or in spite of it—my mom would get into fights with my dad. My brother and mother would fight, and my dad would fight with his second wife. I couldn't get away from the violence. Most of the time it's not teens; it's their parents and families."

There's no denying that some kids are drawn to vio-lence, the way some people are drawn to extreme sports. A few young killers, Grissom and other experts admit, even have the makeup of a sociopath: someone who is incapable of feeling empathy. "Some people don't experience anxiety. What you or I might experience as an uncomfortable feel-ing they perceive as pleasurable."

Kip Kinkel's friends say he bragged about torturing animals—a signal, most experts say, of a kid who is devel-oping homicidal tendencies. Local lore has it that Kip was banned from some of his friends' homes. (Kip was said to have used whipped cream to write "Kill" on their drive-ways.) In January 1997 Kip was busted for dropping a rock onto a car windshield from an overpass—a more violent version of a game lots of kids play: spitting off bridges, toss-ing rocks into a pond. Most kids do these things to get a sense of their own power, to hear the splash of the stone or see the splat of their spit. But with kids like Kip, it's not thrilling enough to exert power over inanimate objects.

It can be hard for teenagers to know how to channel

excess negative energy into positive activities. That's especially true if they don't have the support of a parent or another adult to say, "Hey, let's learn how to sky-dive" or "I'll help you practice so you can make the team." Ron Taffel interviewed about 150 five-, six-, and seven-year-olds for a study published in *Family Therapy Networker*. "Angel-faced innocents," he called them, though their thoughts were not always so innocent. On the contrary, Taffel was very surprised by the level of anger he found even in the five-year-olds, some of whom yelled obscenities at their parents or threw explosive temper tantrums. Taffel concluded that the kids were frustrated by the lack of quality time their parents could give them. In turn, he contended, parents are confused by their kids' anger and don't know how to deal with it: Should they punish the child, or give him more attention, or what? Taffel's theory: There is no easy answer, because each child is his or her own being. One thing was clear to him, though: For kids to feel safe and well adjusted, they need to spend a lot of positive, loving time with their parents. It's not a cure, but it's definitely a start.

Jim, 18 · Mt. Airy, MD

Jim was disciplined growing up, sometimes physically, but he believes that rather than putting him on the wrong path, it kept him on the right one. In fact, he has a happy, loving home life that includes his parents and his two brothers. He also has an adoring girlfriend, likes school, and wants to be a doctor.

I have two brothers: one older, one younger. I was picked on when I was a kid, and I pick on my little brother. I think this is part of growing up. Nobody was ever seriously hurt, and me and my older brother are best friends. People who make a big deal out of a little sibling rivalry are interrupting the growing process.

I think parents should be allowed to discipline their kids and not have to worry if they are abusing them or not. I was spanked as a kid, and not once did I think I didn't deserve it. I always knew what I did wrong, and I learned to respect my parents more because I knew I couldn't get away without a good ass-whupping! I think respect for elders should be stressed in the home and school.

One of my old friends was beaten by his father pretty regularly. His dad was an alcoholic and would punish him for everything that came along with being a kid. Unfortunately, his dad died about two years ago, and my friend's life went to hell. His father was keeping him on the right path in life. Some people choose to raise their kids differently than others. I think that unless someone is seriously hurt, like on the verge of being permanently injured or killed, the government should stay out of family life. They stress the separation of church and state; well, what about home and state?

The school shootings were pretty messed up, but I don't like the older generation's reaction to them. They had to find an excuse for the one in Colorado. Rather than saying those kids were simply screwed up, they blamed TV and music and all those other items.

Kids are part of the messed-up portion of society and they get picked out as being "bad" before they even do anything to deserve that label. People of my generation like to dye their hair and wear baggy clothing and listen to music with explicit lyrics, but that doesn't make them "bad," and they shouldn't be singled out by the previous generation.

Even with really supportive, involved parents, some teens will start fights, torture animals, and kick sand in the face of weaklings. And even if a kid chooses not to be violent, there's nothing to ensure he won't be picked on and riled up by a violent kid, the kind who seems to thrive on starting trouble. Michael Schulman, author of *Bringing Up a Moral Child*, remembers a girl who had started to do very well in his care when, during a field hockey game, she started a huge fight that shut down the event. "I said to her, 'It's a shame that the day ended in a fight,'" Schulman reports. "And she said, 'Oh, the fight was the most fun.'" For some teenagers, fighting gets their adrenaline going, and this may be the only time they really feel alive.

A kid who learns that one way to feel dangerous, sexy, and cool is to make other people feel small or helpless will keep it up. "There are kids who get pleasure out of being cruel," continues Schulman. "A kid can be violent as a way to get things. Or there's violence that emerges out of anger, or betrayal, or a sense of injustice."

But what is injustice to a thirteen-year-old? Getting a B-minus on a test? Getting shoved in a cafeteria line? Getting hazed by a senior? Being publicly teased by a group of ex-friends?

What Are the Signs?

Where were you when you heard about Columbine, Colorado? Twelve students and a teacher were murdered, dozens were injured, and two more kids were dead by their own hand. The killers were smart, well-off kids—who had carefully orchestrated a mass murder. Suddenly school shootings were no longer seen as just a product of the ghetto. For inner-city youths, school violence was old news by the time movies like *Lean on Me* came out in the 1980s. Homicide has been the leading cause of death among African Americans aged fifteen to twenty-four for more than ten years. But now that school violence had begun to bleed into the upper-middle-class communities, the media and the nation were taking notice—and asking whether these crimes could have been prevented.

While administrators usually deny that cliques are a powerful presence in their schools, most students—even those who are in the so-called cool crowd—would beg to differ. Many students felt the Columbine shootings indicated that cliques were a problem, but some students cited actually considered the shootings proof that certain groups deserved to be outcast. And though Dylan Klebold and Eric Harris reportedly sought out jocks in particular during their rampage, Columbine High principal Frank D'Angelo called the existence of jock culture and its role in the shootings a myth.

It's impossible to say who the next school shooter will be. For every Kip and Dylan, Michael and Eric, there are thousands of frustrated, fed-up outsiders. Some will handle the pressure by dropping out of high school. Some will wait it out until they go to college. Others will daydream of being rich and successful so they can show off at the high school reunion; still others will go on feeling bad and never act out at all. But there are also potentially violent kids out there— some bent on revenge. The National School Safety Center has an extensive Web site (www.nsscl.org) dedicated to ending school violence and keeping schools safe. There's no one set of warning signs that guarantee someone will become a killer, but certain things do indicate that a student may snap violently. The NSSC checklist for identifying potentially dangerous students includes:

- Characteristically resorts to name-calling, cursing, or abusive language
- Habitually makes violent threats when angry
- Has a background of serious disciplinary problems at school and in the community
- Has a background of drug, alcohol, or other substance abuse or dependency
- Is on the fringe of his/her peer group with few or no close friends
- Is preoccupied with weapons, explosives, or other incendiary devices
- Has little or no supervision and support from parents or another caring adult
- Has been bullied and/or bullies or intimidates peers or younger children
- Tends to blame others for difficulties and problems s/he causes him/herself
- Prefers TV shows, movies, or music expressing violent themes and acts

- Prefers reading materials dealing with violent themes, rituals, and abuse
- Reflects anger, frustration, and the dark side of life in school essays or writing projects
- Is involved with a gang or an antisocial group on the fringe of peer acceptance
- Is often depressed and/or has significant mood swings

The American Psychological Association also put together a list of warning signs that a kid is likely to become violent. They are:
- Loss of temper on a daily basis
- Frequent physical fighting
- Significant vandalism or property damage
- An increase in use of drugs or alcohol
- Detailed plans to commit acts of violence
- Threats to hurt others
- Enjoyment of hurting animals
- Carrying a weapon

None of this is exactly a news flash—and plenty of violent teens don't meet many of the characteristics outlined above. But if you see any or all of these signs in a classmate or friend, by all means alert a school guidance counselor. Do you find these lists alarming because they describe someone you know—or, perhaps, yourself? Of course they do. Most, if not all, teenagers get moody and depressed and listen to aggressive music, and plenty experiment with drugs. Many write violent poetry or fiction, and most teens (and adults) prefer to blame others for their mistakes. It's not that these lists aren't helpful. A child who continually exhibits much of the behavior cited above may have reason to have his or her well-being questioned. But partly as a result of lists like these, something called geek profiling became an issue following the school shootings.

Kids from all over the country flocked to the gamers site slashdot.org to report what was happening in their schools just after the shootings at Columbine. One kid in Minnesota wrote that he'd been given a choice by his guidance counselor: give up the fantasy game Dungeons and Dragons, which Dylan and Eric had allegedly played, or face counseling and possible suspension. A New York girl complained that the jocks and preppie kids in her school "now have another reason to hate me." Students who were already being excluded and teased wrote that they were now objects of disgust from both students and faculty. Doesn't that just sound like a recipe for making an already alienated kid feel even more alone and angry?

Alix, 17 · Woodstock, CT

Alix is a senior in high school who prides herself on her creative side: She's a good student, but really comes alive in drama productions and the fashion club. She's excited about getting her driver's license. Though growing up hasn't been easy (she says she was unpopular in middle school, and her mother was hospitalized for depression), she considers herself much luckier than some people she knows and credits her good friends with keeping her on track. Still, she worries about school violence—a lot—and hopes to become a youth psychologist to help troubled kids.

When I was younger, my older brother, who is twenty now, had a "problem." He used to love to torment me, and not just in an emotional way. He used to hit me and stuff, and I would never tell my parents, because when I did it got worse. He was the captain of every team ever created, and I was small. He could easily overpower me. It has affected me. To this day I get very timid around people who remind me of him. I back away or just start crying for no reason.

I feel that this country is falling apart. Look at the school shootings. What will happen to our future if the kids are turning out this way? I worry all the time that it could happen at my school. I go to a private school, and it has almost happened several times. Kids at my school have been arrested at school for gun possession with the intent to shoot. Kids ganging together, some with guns, some with bullets. And this is in a small farm town; imagine how it would be in a city. . . . I am glad I am to be in my last year of high school, I just hope I live to see my graduation.

From what I have heard, the kids who shot their classmates were outcasts, or picked on beyond belief. I can relate to that. I was picked on horribly when I was a kid. I can't see myself shooting someone, but there are kids that are driven to do this or they would just explode! I think it is a mental problem, but I'm not sure.

I like the idea of more safety precautions on guns.

Having metal detectors and plastic clear bags aren't the answer. I just think that it backfires. When kids see a challenge, they take it. What has worked in our school is word of mouth. We all have an unspoken agreement that if anything is wrong to a very dangerous level, we tell, and the person who tells is actually made cool. A method we have that could have helped Columbine is the Dr. Black method. In our school, we have no Dr. Black, but if we hear that name on the intercom, then we know that there is a serious problem in the school, and we have been taught how to protect ourselves.

How Can We Stop It?

After the Columbine shootings, many schools developed a zero-tolerance policy when it came to talk of guns, violence, or any kind of weaponry. Students with pictures of guns on their T-shirts were sent home, and kids who made "Bang, bang, you're dead" hand gestures got put on probation. Other students around the country were sent home for wearing trench coats (similar to the ones Dylan Klebold and Eric Harris had used to conceal their weapons), for making threats (for example, "You're so dead"), even for writing poems with violent themes for class assignments. Does such a policy make sense? It seems unlikely that these safety measures will be kept in place forever.

So far, seventeen states have enacted laws decreeing that teens, or in some cases even children, who commit serious crimes can be tried as adults. Thirty-eight states currently authorize the death penalty. Of these, twenty-three allow sixteen- or seventeen-year-olds to receive the death penalty.

On an emotional level, it may sound fair: These kids committed adult crimes, so they should do adult time, the theory goes. But what is our society accomplishing by trying teens as adults? Are we, as psychologist Martin Glasser argues, just satisfying our outrage and our need to punish? After all, he points out, there is usually little question as to the guilt or innocence of teens on trial for violent crimes.

Then there are the stats: Kids placed in adult prisons commit suicide eight times as often as kids in juvenile detention facilities. Kids sentenced to adult prisons are more likely to commit violent crimes when they're released than those sentenced to juvenile institutions. Black kids are more likely to be tried as adults than white kids. Punishing teens by putting them in prison gives them little to no chance of ever becoming functioning members of society. Studies show that kids in adult prisons show few signs of improving their lives once they're released and have a high rate of returning to the justice system.

What *would* help kids on the brink before they commit deadly crimes? The National Longitudinal Study on Adolescent Health found two major factors that reduce violence: school connectedness and family connectedness. Improving family relations may be too big a challenge for society to tackle as a whole, but everyone from the heads of government to the most shy freshman can contribute to making schools safer. If school is a place where you can feel accepted, safe, and encouraged, you're going to feel connected. If school is a place where you don't just sit and listen but speak up and share your ideas, you're going to feel connected. If you're rewarded for participating and being a team player, you're going to feel connected. But if school is somewhere to watch the clock, where kids are ostracized for being different, school becomes a major stressor. And that's when more violence happens.

Parents can help by getting more involved with schools and pushing for changes that will bring about a positive learning and social environment—as opposed to the jockocracy that exists in so many schools today. Teens can help by standing up for values they believe in, peer-policing those who are mean to others, and being accepting of everyone.

"Yeah, violence in the media affects teens. I love martial arts and fighting games, so I decided, Hey, why don't I take up karate?" says a sixteen-year-old girl. "I myself have seriously thought of taking a weapon into class and killing some people because they made me so mad. In fact, at one point the only problem was lack of a gun. When you look at me, I'm an average 'jeans and a T-shirt' suburbanite. But I'm more likely to hurt someone than the goth girl who sits behind me in math. The media stereotypes teen killers as wearing all black (trench coats) and constantly being on drugs . . . but usually we kill or hurt others just because our feelings are hurt or there's some aspect of life we feel we would be better off without. What people need to do is stop talking about it and start acting. See someone sitting alone? Say hi! If a good student suddenly starts failing, the teacher should talk to the guidance counselor about it. If a parent notices a child acting strange, *get him into therapy*. Many schools *have* a therapist their students can visit during free periods. The point is, anyone off the street could be ready to kill you, and I'll bet it's not one of the ones wearing black plastic pants and lots of makeup. I go to a rich, small high school where we've already had two or three suicides and a Columbine-ish scare, all by people we thought would never do it . . . straight-A students and the leader of the morning Bible study."

Andrea, 17 · Pittsfield, MA
Andrea calls her group of friends the "smart kids," not as obsessed with popularity as the in clique, not so much on the fringes as the goths. She's more excited about getting into college than she is worried about making it out of high school.

Some teachers try to help kids who get teased. Elementary school teachers try to help, but teachers don't help much when you're in high school.

Last year at the end of school there was a student who had threatened to kill a teacher. It wasn't widely known, but my teacher mentioned it to me. The guidance counselors were really watching that child, and the parents and teachers were a little bit edgy.

Anything is possible. I would never think that I have that choice—to actually shoot other people. Because there are so many other ways to handle things. There are certain kids who get teased all throughout elementary school for different things. Like for being different. Kids who don't dress like everyone else or who don't have the money to buy the clothes like everyone else—those kids get teased.

My best friend and I talked about different school shootings when they happened. Overall, the consensus was: It was a tragedy. You never know, it could happen in our school. You think it could, but you never think it actually will. I don't feel scared.

Maybe those kids felt it was their only way to handle what they were feeling. I don't know what would drive a person to that point. I guess letting your anger get out of control. They'll probably go to jail or some juvenile detention, when they really need help instead. Something has to be mentally wrong with you if you get to that point. A person who can shoot up a school needs to figure out why he acted that way, and I don't know if it's something he can accomplish while in jail. Jail may punish you, but when you get out of jail, are you going to be changed, or are you going to do the same thing again?

I think those kids think they won't go to jail. Jail's not a deterrent because I don't think those people think about it when they're about to do something wrong. What crook thinks he's going to get caught before he robs a house? It's been proven that crime does not drop in a state because of the death penalty. People don't think, "Am I going to go to jail? Am I going to get the death penalty if I do this and I get caught?"

The truth is, violence as a whole is decreasing, but the proportion of violent crime committed by juveniles is much higher than their criminal behavior as a whole. And despite the recent rash of school shootings, on-campus violence is actually down too.

Some kids have always had access to guns; in fact, the National Rifle Association recommends teaching children the proper care and firing of a gun as soon as they're old enough to wield one. And kids have always been exposed to violence—if not on the screen, then in their homes or communities. You know kids are cruel. The news that Michael Carneal's Paducah, Kentucky, classmates humiliated him and teased him didn't surprise anyone. And if you are or ever have been a teen, you know the true meaning of the phrase "raging hormones." It's not just about feeling sexed up—there's also the confusion, the elation, the depression, and the anger, all of which seem to spring rapidly to the surface at the slightest provocation.

And the volume on everything that makes the teen years dangerous has been turned way up: The violence in movies and on TV is extreme, and the Federal Trade Commission has found that the most extremely violent video games, movies, and TV shows are marketed toward teens. The news reports of violence are vastly disproportionate to the amount of actual violence, because the networks know that violence captures viewers. Guns are bigger, faster, better killing machines. Teens are more sophisticated, more savvy, and yes, perhaps more cruel and hotheaded. Add this to the developmental stage teens are in, and the question really isn't How did this happen? but Why isn't this happening more often? Think about it: Do you know a Michael Carneal, a Kip Kinkel, a Dylan Klebold? Someone who gets dumped on, teased mercilessly, constantly left out? Do you know someone who lurks in the background, maybe quietly seething, looking for anyone or anything over which he can wield control? You bet you do. Be careful how you treat him.

Teens Who Kill

March 2001 · San Diego, California

A fifteen-year-old student allegedly brings a .22 caliber revolver to his high school in his backpack. He loads the gun in the boys' restroom and begins shooting students at random, leaving two teenagers dead and thirteen people wounded. Students described him as a kid who was often bullied—a classmate told the *Columbus Dispatch*, "People called him freak, dork, nerd—stuff like that." At press time, the alleged shooter had not entered a plea and it had not been decided if he would be tried as a juvenile or an adult.

January 2001 · Etna, New Hampshire

Two males, sixteen and seventeen, allegedly enter the home of Half and Suzanne Zantop (both Dartmouth College professors) and stab them in their heads, necks, and chests until both are dead. The two teachers are discovered by a friend a few hours later when she comes over for pre-arranged dinner plans. The teens' trial was pending at press time.

February 2000 · Brooklyn, New York

Lavar Davis, seventeen, enters a deli in Flatbush along with a friend, nineteen. Both have loaded guns. When the shopkeeper ducks behind the counter instead of giving up the $62 in his register, Davis shoots and kills him. At the friend's trial in February 2001, Davis, who is sentenced to fifteen years to life in prison, testifies that his friend forced him into the robbery by threatening to kill him if he didn't participate.

April 1999 · Littleton, Colorado

Columbine High School seniors Eric Harris and Dylan Klebold open fire in their school with automatic weapons. As a result, twelve students and one teacher are killed and more than twenty people are wounded. The two gunmen then committed suicide. A teacher told *60 Minutes* reporter Ed Bradley that Harris looked at her, smiled, then shot her in the shoulder.

May 1998 · Springfield, Oregon

Kip Kinkel, fifteen, walks into his school with two guns he'd been given by his father and starts shooting. Two Thurston High students die; twenty are wounded. As he's being arrested, Kip pulls a knife and lunges at the police officer. Police later find his parents murdered at home. Kip is tried as an adult and sentenced to 112 years in prison.

May 1998 · Clearfield, Pennsylvania

Jessica Nicole Holtmeyer, sixteen, her then-fiancé, and nine other teens hang an unpopular girl, fifteen, in a wooded area. Holtmeyer and her fiancé then bludgeon her in the face with a baseball-sized rock until she dies. Jessica is sentenced to life in prison.

April 1998 · Edinboro, Pennsylvania

A fourteen-year-old boy takes his dad's pistol and shoots up a middle school dance. He kills a teacher and wounds two students and another teacher. Previously, he had told kids that he wanted to be like the kids in Arkansas. He is tried as an adult.

December 1997 · Paducah, Kentucky

Michael Carneal, fourteen, opens fire on his high school prayer circle. Three teenage girls die; five other teens are wounded. He is tried as an adult. He pleads guilty but mentally ill; he will be in jail for at least twenty-five years. Carneal tells psychiatrists that students called him a faggot. The first person shot was a girl he allegedly had a crush on.

October 1997 · Pearl, Mississippi

Luke Woodham, sixteen, kills his mother, then goes to school and shoots nine students. Two die; seven are injured. Five months before, he had allegedly tied up his dog, Sparkle, in a plastic bag, taken her into the woods, and pummeled her. He then doused the bag with lighter fluid, set it aflame, and sank Sparkle in a pond. After being tried for the shootings as an adult, Luke is sentenced to life in prison. On his confession tape, he says, "People always picked on me. They called me gay and stupid stuff like that. I guess the world's going to remember me now. I'm probably gonna get pretty famous."

June 1997 · New York, New York

Corey Arthur, nineteen, goes over to his teacher Jonathan Levin's apartment, tortures him with a knife, and shoots him in the head. He is currently serving twenty-five years to life in prison.

May 1997 · Long Beach, California

Jeremy Strohmeyer, eighteen, follows a seven-year-old girl into a restroom while on vacation in Nevada. There he sexually assaults and strangles her, then reportedly returns to celebrating the long weekend with his friends. He pleads guilty and is sentenced to life in prison.

May 1997 · New York, New York

Daphne Abdela, fifteen, daughter of a New York City millionaire, and Christopher Vasquez, fifteen, are partying in Central Park after dark with a forty-four-year-old real estate agent. They go for a walk with him, stab him more than thirty times, and, at Daphne's suggestion, disembowel him in the hope that the body will sink when they toss it into a nearby pond. It does not; Abdela

SCARY STATS

Almost three million crimes occur on or near school property every year.

U.S. DEPARTMENT OF JUSTICE

The number of students age twelve to nineteen reporting violent crime at school in 1989 was 3.4 million; by 1995 it was 4.2 million.

U.S. BUREAU OF JUSTICE

Between 1989 and 1994, the number of homicide arrests among children age ten to fourteen increased 41 percent, and 18 percent among those age eighteen to twenty-four. Late in 1996, though, the U.S. Justice Department reported a decline in the number of arrests for violent crimes among those younger than fifteen, suggesting the rate may have peaked.

U.S. DEPARTMENT OF JUSTICE

reports the body to the police, say-ing Vasquez killed the man. Abdela eventually admits her role in the murder and pleads guilty; Vasquez has a jury trial. Both are convicted of first-degree manslaughter.

April 1997 · Franklin, New Jersey

Thomas Koskovich, eighteen, and Jason Vreeland, seventeen, call sev-eral pizza places until one agrees to send a delivery to a remote cabin. When the two deliverymen arrive, Vreeland and Koskovich fire at least eight shots into them. Koskovich is sentenced to death; Vreeland faces life in prison.

March 1997 · Jonesboro, Arkansas

Andrew Golden, eleven, pulls the fire alarm at his school. He runs to the nearby woods where Mitchell Johnson, thirteen, is hiding with enough gunpower and ammunition to kill hundreds. Moments later, the two open fire on students and teach-ers who are streaming out of the Westside Middle School. Four female students and one teacher are killed; ten other students are wounded. The two are tried as juveniles and will be in state custody until they are twenty-one.

January 1997 · Seattle, Washington

Two eighteen-year-old males are arrested and charged with strangling a twenty-year-old woman in a park. They then kill her parents and her sister, seventeen, in the family's home. One of the alleged killers later reports that he just wanted to kill someone because he was "in a rut."

February 1996 · Moses Lake, Washington

A fourteen-year-old uses an assault weapon on his ninth-grade algebra class, killing two students and one teacher. One of the targets is a popular boy who had teased him. According to the *New York Times*, the assailant stood over a dying boy who was choking on his own blood and said, "This sure beats algebra, doesn't it?"

America has the highest rates of childhood homicide, suicide, and firearm-related death among industrialized countries. The homicide rate for kids under fifteen is five times higher than that for children of other industrialized nations.

CDC

Ten percent of public schools had one or more incidents of violent crime during the 1996–1997 school year.

NATIONAL CENTER OF EDUCATION STATISTICS

" I don't think people realize how serious a problem teen
suicide, depression, and general mental anguish is. More
people hide it than you might think. I don't feel I am very
attractive. During high school, I had guys tell me I was fat
and ugly to my face.

So how does this relate to teen suicide? When I am told by
my peers and by my culture that I am not good enough, am I to feel I
am worth the effort it takes to breathe? Being told you are a loser
can rip your soul into shreds. Here I am, a depressed nineteen-year-
old college sophomore, attempting to gain a sense of self-worth
in a world that wants to chew me up and spit me out without a
moment of regret. Being a shy virgin in college oftentimes is almost
looked at as being a curse. I know that there are people out there
who think people like me are wise, or strong, who would praise

us. But there are others who call us losers because we haven't had boyfriends or girlfriends and don't meet the social standards set by our peers.

Several months ago, I attempted to kill myself and was saved by friends who cared. I merely wish people to know that suicide is not a minor issue. I think because of the social stigma that accompanies death by one's own hand, the issue gets pushed to the back burner.

Several years ago, Pearl Jam released a song called 'Jeremy.' The video depicted a high school boy shooting up a class of students who constantly ridiculed him. I find that I can relate to this song and video, and others should take it as a reminder that a person's surroundings and peers have a greater impact than one might think. We are human beings, not machines. A person can only take so much before reaching a breaking point."

—Jill, 19

Chapter 2

No Going Back:
Teen Suicide

Randall James was the kind of kid other kids pick on—classmates say he was tortured, scapegoated, and scorned. Seniors would tease the North Richland, Texas, sixteen-year-old, then shout, "Run, Randall, run!" after him. People even remember him crying in the halls. Of course, there are millions of other students for whom high school is a living hell—including plenty of computer lovers and wise guys, both of which Randall reportedly was. What set Randall apart was his decision that he wasn't going to take it anymore. On January 22, 1999, Randall ended his torment. That morning he went to school, locked himself in a bathroom stall, and shot himself with a 9-millimeter gun.

In any high school cafeteria, you can find a kid like Randall: He's the one sitting alone, pushing his food around with a spork, staring into the middle distance. Or maybe there's a high-strung girl who seems popular, but you wonder if she has a real best friend. Or a guy who's getting into trouble at school, at home, maybe even with the police. You might not notice him in homeroom—he sits in the back and doesn't talk much. You might not notice him on the bus, sitting alone, staring out the window. You might not notice him at all . . . until he's gone.

Then again, the next kid to kill himself might not be an obviously sad introvert like Randall. He may be popular, outgoing, and part of the in crowd, someone like Rob Pace, who was an eighteen-year-old at Riverhead High School in Mineola, New York. Rob was an honor student, involved in his city's youth court, and a varsity athlete. On April 14, 2000, Rob traveled with his class to an amusement park in New Jersey. Like many teens, Rob dabbled in drugs, and that day he was carrying marijuana, ecstasy, and coke. He was busted going into the park; school officials sent him home. On the train ride home, Rob put a note on his seat that read, "Please tell anyone who ever knew me that 'I'm sorry for letting them down!'" Then he jumped to his death between two train cars.

The next teenager to commit suicide might not be someone who's facing a trauma, like being arrested. It could be someone whose life seems perfect. Julie Nadybal was a fifteen-year-old whose only troubles seemed to come from within. From the outside, Julie appeared an enviable eighth grader: pretty, an honor student, a member of the flag team, a ballerina, and a poet, popular and friendly. But the Cobb County, Georgia, teen had struggled for months with what doctors labeled depression, and an eating disorder, and obsessive-compulsive disorder (OCD). Then there were suicide attempts (one that her family didn't even know about until they read her diary, called "My Little Book of Secrets"). Asked on a questionnaire what she'd like to change about herself, she gave the following answer: "To numb my extreme sensitivity and emotions."

Julie's family took her to more than ten doctors in an attempt to help her. She even tried several medications. But in May 1998, her younger brother found her hanging by a belt (he'd gone into her room to ask her how to spell the word "consequences"). "The dancer I should have been missed out on life," Julie wrote in a poem. "She was passionate about dancing alone. Unfortunately she did not remove her blinders to see what life has to offer."

What's Going On Here?

Almost everyone thinks about suicide at some point. It's normal to think about the power you have, including the power to end your own life. So if you've had thoughts like "I'd be better off dead," it doesn't necessarily mean there's something seriously wrong with you. But why do some teens just have a fleeting thought or two about suicide, while others plot to end their own lives or even actually pull the trigger? People who study suicide say it's got something to do with the kind of person you are, and a little to do with the circumstances you're in.

While teen suicide isn't exactly common, it is a significant problem in this country: The government estimates that about 275,000 teens try to kill themselves each year. Statistics show that teens turn to suicide more often than adults: While there are 25 attempts on average for every completed adult suicide, there are 100 to 200 attempts by young people on average for every completed suicide.

Joanie, 18 · Austin, TX

Joanie's biggest problem is fitting it all in: She cheered on the school squad until recently, hangs out with a fun group of people, works after school in a restaurant, participates in her local teen court, partners with special-education kids in a learning program, and still finds the time to make school her number one priority. Her parents are psychologists, and she especially loves the social sciences. But she faces challenges also: She has a learning disorder, and she's had to deal with the death of two friends— one in an accident, the other a suicide.

I think it's hard to be a teenager—there's a lot going on today that's horrible. The things I watch on the news: kids shooting kids in school, bringing drugs and guns to school . . . my school is not like that. The worst we have is the sheriff's deputy walking around at a football game. I don't do a lot of what my friends do, but I have remained friends with them while they go through it; they're getting involved with drugs, going to jail.

Both my parents are professional counselors. I take medication for ADD; it is harder than people think. I get depressed; I let things get me down a lot. I don't have any best friends right now. I thought I had the best friends in the world, but one day someone said something to them that wasn't true, and so they started talking about me and putting me down and talking dirty behind my back. I got depressed about that. I had them come over to my house, but then I told them they couldn't come into my house, so we stood outside and I put everything that I had of theirs in a bag for them, and I was like, "Here's your stuff, I don't want you to be here." We're sort of friends again now; I forgave them—that's the right thing to do. We act just like we used to, but I feel different. I'm never going to tell them anything that's important—I don't trust them now.

I quit cheerleading because of that, plus cheerleading was a bit too much for me. I had done it for four years—it kind of gets old. Also I was working as a waitress and I do teen court. I'm a juror. We mainly get cases about vandalism, minor theft, shooting out streetlights with BB guns, a kid stealing a salad from school.

Joe, who was a good friend of mine, died because of drunk driving, and I was real sad. It surprised me, 'cause I thought he was smarter than that. He wasn't driving, Billy was driving, and Billy killed himself a little while after Joe died. He was being charged with manslaughter, and he killed himself. I lost two of them there. I wasn't as good friends with Billy, but it was still scary, still weird that he killed himself. They were eighteen and nineteen; this was just a couple of months ago. I didn't get to go to any of the funerals because "Cheerleading comes first," they said—we had a competition coming up. That's another reason why I quit cheerleading. I was sick of them throwing that in my face. My life comes first.

One of my friends, the guy I'm dating now, we've

been dating almost two months but we're not really going together, or however you want to call it—we're not classifying it. He told me what happened to Billy. I didn't believe it—God, how many rumors go around after something like that? We sat out on the driveway and talked about it. I don't cry in front of anybody; all I could say was "Oh my God, wow." I didn't know what to do. I went home and cried about it, but I wasn't going to let him see me crying.

I didn't want to know how he killed himself. He thought the world was over. I mean, he killed his best friend. It was everyone's fault who was there: Billy's fault to drive while drinking and Joe's fault for deciding to get into the car with someone who had been drinking. They went into a culvert and flipped over. Joe died right away. Billy killed himself a couple of weeks later.

I think he did the wrong thing. There's always a reason to live. God gave life to you—what right do you have to take it away? I'm not one of those people who believes that if you kill yourself you're going to hell. It's your life and you can do what you want to, but no matter how bad things get, there's always a reason to live your life out. Who knows what was in your future? I think that I would have taken the punishment they had for me—most punishments fit the crime.

If a suicide is in a newspaper, it's okay if all they're doing is giving facts. I don't think they should refer to Romeo and Juliet, though. Did you hear about that? A Hispanic couple I read about in a teen magazine, a boy and girl, neither of them could swim, and their parents wouldn't let them see each other so they jumped in a river together and drowned. They were calling it the Romeo and Juliet story. I don't think they should do that.

Why would anyone take such an extreme measure as suicide instead of talking out problems or trying to find a solution, *any* other solution? Suicide is often referred to as "a permanent solution to a temporary problem." That's because people who are supersad may feel that their only choice is to kill themselves. But just because suicide can seem like the only solution doesn't mean that it is. The truth is, there are always lots of options in life, it's just a matter of helping people identify them. But a teenager who feels isolated may not have someone to help him or her see the other options available.

"Teens have no one to talk to," writes one girl, and many others echo the idea that teenagers feel alone, with no one they can confide in—no one who really understands them.

"Teens take this way out because they have many problems and they feel this is the only way out," writes a fifteen-year-old girl from Chesterland, Ohio. "They are confused and scared. They also usually try to tell someone that they are having problems before they die." A teen whose family puts a lot of pressure on him to excel may have a hard time figuring out a backup plan for if, say, he gets cut from the basketball team or gets a C in Spanish or doesn't get into his college of choice. A teen who's constantly in trouble, on the other hand, may view suicide as the only way out of the disciplinary actions he's expecting.

A number of teenagers name "To get back at someone" as a possible reason for committing suicide. Logically, this almost makes sense: Someone lets you down, hurts you, or makes you feel small, and you want to get back at them, big time, so you figure you'll put the weight of your death on their shoulders. Right? Well, you know how a little kid "hides" from you by covering his eyes (he can't see you, so he figures you can't see him, either)? In a way, teenagers go through a phase in which they apply the same kind of reasoning. Intellectually, you know that once you're dead, you can't point at your enemies and go "Ha! I showed you!" But a part of you still wants to believe that you can.

"Teenagers often don't fully understand life and death," says Ruth Mikkelson, who has been principal in the Court and Community Schools in Marysville, California, for nine years. "They don't realize that no one cares if you kill yourself." This sounds a little harsh, but what Mikkelson is saying is that if you kill yourself, your parents will be horrified and your friends will be traumatized and your school may hold a minute of silence for you the following Monday. But the sad fact of life is it goes on, no matter who's alive or dead. People mourn and grieve, but at some point, whether it's a week or a year or a few years later, they move on. A suicide death will affect people deeply—for a limited time. A well-lived life is shared and remembered by those close to you for up to a century, and you can affect people at different times in myriad ways, even if you do hit a few rough spots along the way.

"And," continues Mikkelson, "[suicidal] teens don't

realize that you only have one life—you don't get to come back. You don't get to watch yourself at your funeral." Or witness your classmates mourning you, or see your parents fall apart, or find out whether your best friend really is sorry. You're just dead.

Who's Doing This?

"Four out of five teenagers who commit suicide are boys," says Dr. David Shaffer, a professor of pediatrics and psychiatry at Columbia University, who has studied adolescent suicide for over two decades. "About ninety or ninety-two percent of them have a psychiatric disorder," he adds. Though the vast majority of completed teen suicides are boys, girls attempt suicide way more often: The American Association of Suicidology puts the ratio at 3 to 1. This might have something to do with the suicide method of choice: Girls tend to turn to less lethal methods such as poison, cutting, or hanging themselves, whereas boys often use guns.

We can look at the stats to see who's at risk (boys more than girls, depressed teens more than teens who aren't depressed), but even that information can't always help us figure out who will end his or her own life. "This phenomenon is very difficult for anyone to predict," warns Thomas Joiner, associate professor of psychology at Florida State University and former director of youth psychological assessment at the Department of Psychiatry at the University of Texas, Galveston. "A lot of the emotional and psychopathological precursors to suicide are not at all visible. People can harbor pretty intense depression and not show it."

In other words, someone who seems perfectly normal to you one day can become suicidal the next, especially during the emotionally intense teen years. This is not to say that you should be paranoid about your friends committing suicide: It's still a relatively rare occurrence. But if someone you know does kill himself or herself, you can't automatically assume that you should have known or that you missed the signs. Sometimes there simply are no signs, or there are things that happened that were obvious signs after the fact but didn't seem out of the ordinary at the time.

"I know that even I, a girl who loves life beyond pretty much anything, have thought about suicide," writes a fourteen-year-old girl. "Teens are in the midst of a massive hormone rush; we are exploring life. Something traumatic almost always manages to drill its way into your life when you are a teen. So who wouldn't think of suicide?"

Some of the risk factors for suicide are pretty obvious: Teenagers who are clinically depressed or have another psychological disorder are more likely to kill themselves, as are teens who are under a ton of stress, particularly family-related stress. Usually it's a combination of factors: depression, a superstressful period (such as final exams or when parents are fighting), and, often, a trigger event.

A trigger event might be a big fight, or parents' divorce, or anything that feels like a personal failure (like getting in trouble, bombing a midterm, or being cut from a team). Most teenagers can withstand life's disappointments without feeling the urge to harm themselves, but some teens find it hard to see what options are available to them beyond suicide, especially if they are under a lot of stress or clinically depressed. There are some teens experts have determined are most at risk for suicide:

Teens with Depression You probably hear people say "I'm so depressed" all the time. This is usually not the same as clinical depression, which is an illness that can strike anyone, at any age. At first, it can be hard to differentiate between people who are clinically depressed and people who might actually attempt suicide. The easiest way to think of it is that depression is a condition, but suicide is a decision. Certainly, depression sometimes influences people to decide to try to kill themselves—but there are also cases of suicide in which the person wasn't depressed, and millions of clinically depressed people who never try to harm themselves.

Depression is a dangerous thing—it's linked to thirty thousand suicides in America every year. About nineteen million adults (one in twenty people) are estimated to have depression each year. If you're depressed as a teen, you're more likely to be depressed as an adult—that's why it's important for depressed teens to get treatment.

Clinical depression makes people feel down and sad regardless of what's going on in their lives. With depression, even if things are going great (you're getting good grades, your parents are being cool about letting you drive, you have great friends), you might still feel sad and not know why. Depression can also bring feelings of loneliness, isolation (you feel like no one could ever understand you, no one cares about you), and hopelessness about your future (you think you'll never feel happy again).

To be even more specific, the National Institute of

Mental Health has flagged these symptoms in people who have depression:

- **Persistent sad or "empty" mood.** For instance, your friend has stopped talking and laughing with you during class breaks. Instead, he or she seems sullen and withdrawn.
- **Feelings of hopelessness and pessimism that don't go away.** Maybe you hear a friend saying negative things, like "It doesn't really matter, I'll never be good at anything anyway."
- **Loss of interest or pleasure in hobbies and activities the person used to enjoy.** This is easy to identify and almost certainly signals a problem. For example, you once loved being on the volleyball team or singing in choir, but now the thought of these activities just makes you tired, not excited—as if they're chores.
- **Insomnia or oversleeping.** Napping after school, sleeping all day on the weekends, going to bed very early or waking up before the crack of dawn—any unusual sleep patterns like these could be symptomatic of depression.
- **Tired or sluggish feeling.** Sometimes people who have depression report that they feel like they're moving in slow motion or that their body feels much heavier—like it takes a big effort to move even a few steps.
- **Restlessness, irritability.** Take notice if a formerly even-tempered friend becomes cranky and easily annoyed.
- **Hard time concentrating, remembering, or making decisions.** Decisions that didn't seem like a big deal a few months ago (like what to have for lunch, or where to hang out after school) can seem overwhelming to a depressed person.

- *Crying a lot.* Sobbing and not knowing why, or going on a crying jag over something minor like a sappy TV commercial.
- *Persistent physical symptoms, like a stomachache or headache that doesn't seem to get better even after treatment.* Depressed people often have a heightened sensitivity to pain, so what most people perceive as a minor "ouch," such as a paper cut or banged knee, can make a depressed person feel really wounded.
- *Thoughts of death or suicide.* It's not true that people who talk about suicide won't ever do it. Lots of people who have committed suicide did mention it to friends or family members before they actually attempted it. It's important to listen to what friends say, as well as to pay attention to your own intuition. A comment like "Well, I'll be dead before this project is due anyway" could be a clue that becomes obvious only after a tragedy has happened.

An annoying thing about depression is that it can often look like the depressed person is just being lazy. She might choose to nap, for instance, instead of dealing with the world around her. Depressed people are also incredibly self-focused. Oftentimes they'll stop calling friends or going out. A depressed girl may choose to be alone in her room instead of joining the family for dinner. Or she might procrastinate, staring blankly at the television, or even just sitting and doing nothing for hours on end instead of doing homework or studying for an upcoming test. These behaviors can trigger negative reactions from family ("Oh, she's in one of her moods; she won't deign to join us for dinner") and friends ("She blew us off again?!"). These negative reactions can then make the depressed person even more depressed, as she realizes her friends and family are getting bored or fed up with her incessantly cranky mood, so it's a vicious cycle.

The symptoms of depression can last weeks, months, or even years. When it's not addressed, depression can cause anxiety attacks, headaches—and increase your susceptibility to long-term illness. It can also kill you. When depression is caught early, 80 percent of patients with symptoms of depression show a marked improvement. But getting help can be difficult, especially for teenagers.

"If an adult is suffering from clinical depression, it's viewed as a medical problem, which it is," says a sixteen-year-old girl. "When a teenager is depressed, regardless of his or her cries for help, it's simply dismissed as teenage angst. I will not deny that puberty is an angst-filled time, but some cases of teenage angst really ought to be examined more closely. I know whereof I speak in this case; I've been diagnosed with dysthymia (severe long-term depression) and a few other select disorders. It sickens and saddens me that people very close to me have made attempts to end their own lives and scarcely anyone so much as raised an eyebrow. 'It's just the age; you'll get over it.' When? Surely we may seem moody and irritable, but no parent should ever fear their own child. I just sincerely wish more parents could talk to their kids. If their teen needs help, for God's sake admit it and get them help. There is no shame in seeking help for someone who needs it."

There are plenty of cases in which a young person's depression goes unnoticed, and friends or family just chalk it up to his being "moody" or "quiet." But one study found that about 50 percent of youth who committed suicide had seen a health care provider in the month before, and 25 percent in the week before. Not every doctor asks teens questions about depression during yearly physicals, but all signs indicate that they should. Short of going to the doctor's office, there are tons of ways a person shows he or she is depressed. But these signals are often missed, in part because parents may deny that their child has depression, even after a positive diagnosis. Parents may be afraid of what other people will say about their kid or, worse yet, about their own parenting style; or they're skeptical of psychological diagnoses in general. So even if a teen asks for help, it's not always enough.

"My best friend started refusing to eat anything that wasn't fat-free, got bad headaches, and started to bruise easily," writes a thirteen-year-old girl. "I started noticing she was depressed. I have clinical depression and am on meds, so I know what depression feels and looks like. Then she started to call me, sobbing. She was suicidal. I was scared for her. I didn't know what to do, plus she was hurting herself with nail clippers, scratching herself with them. So I did what seemed right at the time: I saw my school counselor. She did nothing. This was a matter of my best friend's *life*. Finally, the counselor called my friend's parents. Guess what they did? Counseling? Doctor's visit? *Nothing!* They just didn't get it."

Anxious Teens Large numbers of teens who commit suicide do not suffer from depression. These teens may have an anxiety disorder that is undiagnosed, according to Dr.

David Shaffer. Because anxious kids try so hard to be liked, they are often very popular in school. Since they seem fine, they are rarely sent for counseling.

"There are a lot of very suicidal people who are not depressed or impulsive," says Thomas Joiner. "A big factor seems to be intense anxiety or panic disorder."

For teens with an anxiety disorder, "the anxiety is always there," says Joiner. "It's painful and chronic, and some people just reach their threshold in terms of how much psychological pain they're willing to put up with."

More than nineteen million Americans suffer from anxiety disorders. These include panic disorders (sudden bursts of intense fear, as well as possible dizziness, chest pain, and heart palpitations), obsessive-compulsive disorder (people with OCD constantly repeat the same rituals, like checking the door locks twenty-five times a night or washing their hands in a specific complicated way before they eat). Others include post-traumatic stress disorder (blackouts or flashbacks following a traumatic life event like a car wreck), phobias, and generalized anxiety disorder (constant abnormal worry that affects daily life).

"People misunderstand these kids and think that the parents put too much pressure on them," says Dr. David Shaffer, "but often when you speak to the family members you learn that the pressure is coming from inside the kid." So that's a new factor to look out for: someone who appears overly anxious or panicked about grades, friends—everything.

Gay Teens No chapter about teen suicide could be written without addressing the issues of gay and lesbian teens. A

1989 U.S. Department of Health and Human Services study found that lesbian and gay youth are two to three times more likely to attempt suicide than straight kids. In fact, lesbian and gay kids account for roughly 30 percent of all teen suicides.

In a culture in which it's still often considered a slur to be called gay, it's no wonder gay kids have a hard time in high school. When the word is flung around at girls for cutting their hair short—or at guys for letting theirs grow long, speaking with a lilting inflection, having the wrong hobbies, or dropping a football pass—it makes sense that many gay teens keep their sexual preference a secret. In a 1997 Youth Risk Behavior Study among Massachusetts high school students, 46 percent of the gay, lesbian, and bisexual students said they had attempted suicide, compared with 8.8 percent of students in general.

"I'm bi, and I know a lot of people who can't deal with gays," writes a fourteen-year-old girl. "Society forces people into automatically assuming they're straight, but the number of gay teens is bigger than you might think. I'm only out to one of my friends. It's not an easy thing to deal with, because it seems like just one more thing that makes me different from everybody else. There's a lot of attention in the media and stuff about gay issues, but it's all directed at adults. I think more teens should get involved in talking about this because I think it's on a lot of our minds, and it's not 'just a phase,' as so many parents want to believe."

As tolerance for gay and lesbian youth in this country increases (and more gay teens come to realize that life does get easier after high school), we can hope that fewer gay and lesbian teenagers will feel isolated, despondent, and depressed enough to commit suicide. Steps are being taken in that direction already. Perhaps the best example is the group Parents and Friends of Lesbians and Gays. PFLAG is an organization that helps promote tolerance and understanding among parents and friends of homosexuals. There are PFLAG chapters all over the country and confidential meetings that take place every week. For more information, go to www.pflag.org. Many teens in large cities also have access to teen centers directed at gay, lesbian, and bi youths.

Ted, 18 · Santa Fe, NM

Ted knows what it's like to worry about being called names, taunted, and worse. He lives in a wealthy suburb of Santa Fe and goes to a private school where athletes rule, and he doesn't feel safe disclosing his true identity (as a gay teenager) to anyone—not even his parents. He describes himself as a drama geek and says he can't wait until he can move to New York City and become an exotic dancer.

My school is really uptight. We kind of live in a Bible Belt type of town. There's not much personal freedom allowed. Sports are the main thing, which I'm not into. I'm into the arts. I like abstract painting, and I'm in choir, drama, dance—all that.

Cliques are a big deal at my school. You have the skater druggies, then you have the superpopular kids, the junkies, the jocks, the kind of high-class sluts, and then the low-class sluts, who everyone hates but I think they're kind of cool—they're honest. Then you have the artistic people and the freaks.

I once went into the hospital for attempting suicide. I'm bipolar—we just found that out, so I have medication for it now, but one time I was at home, and I slit my wrist. I was sixteen. I still have the scars. And the other time I just OD'd on allergy medicine and some of my parents' medications. When I woke up I was throwing up blood.

I'm gay, and it doesn't surprise me that gay teenagers try suicide more often than straight ones. The hard thing about it is that half of the superpopular people I know, I've been with. And that's one thing about high school: Everything is so hidden. Being gay is a whole different kind of loneliness. I don't know if my parents know or not; I'm private when it comes to sex. There are some things that people don't need to know.

I don't know why I attempted suicide—it was like a lot of things all just kind of piled up. I had a friend die of AIDS, so that was bad, but that wasn't the main thing. The main thing was I slept with someone and got really attached, but he had a significant other, so I couldn't have him. I have friends, but I just can't relate to a lot of them. I basically felt there was nothing for me in the world, and what was the point? For a while, I was disappointed that I didn't die.

Of course, my parents were horrified. I basically played it off, though—we don't really talk about it. I don't want to talk to them about it. I mean, they'd be helpful, but I think they'd try to do the wrong things, like psychiatry—I tried that before, for a year, and I hated it. It's so clinical and generalized, like I don't think you can really generalize problems like that. I thought it was really cheesy, although I have friends that really like it.

I'm looking forward to graduating and moving to New York City. I got invited to audition at Juilliard, but I don't want to go to college. I have friends who go to NYU, and I'm getting an apartment with them. First I'll get some cheesy waiter job, then I told my parents I want to strip. I thought it might be fun. Not fun . . . but interesting.

The Cluster Phenomenon In the book and movie *The Virgin Suicides*, one girl in a small town kills herself, only to have her four sisters follow her path. That's made up, but the phenomenon isn't: All across the country, communities have dealt with the terrible blow of copycat suicides, in which young people kill themselves one after another. Since the late 1980s, forty-nine clusters have occurred, including Westchester County, New York; South Boston, Massachusetts; Bergenfield, New Jersey; and Plano, Texas.

When fifteen-year-old Kenny White shot himself with his father's gun in December 1997, it was the eighth teen suicide in Pierre, South Dakota, in three years. Kenny seemed relatively happy; that day, he'd eaten with a friend and bought some Christmas presents. In his suicide note, he blamed peer pressure and hinted at being upset with a couple of teachers. He also asked his separated parents to get back together. Before that, it had been Michelle Cox, a troubled teen who stayed home from church one day and killed herself with her parents' gun. And John Bartel. And five others—most seemingly happy, healthy kids, some of whom had even talked about how they could never kill themselves. The national suicide rate is 13 per 100,000 people, but in Pierre it's 72 per 100,000. It's such an overreaching problem that eighteen-year-old Alison Friez ran for and won the position of student vice president using the platform "Let's get help to stop all these teen suicides." The same strategy helped her later go on to become Miss Teen South Dakota.

What's the deal with cluster suicides? "The first event stimulates suicidal thinking," says Alan Berman of the American Association of Suicidology. "Others are susceptible, and they use the first person as a permission giver. This shows them they will get a certain amount of attention with death." This could explain why some studies show that for a few weeks after a highly publicized suicide, suicide rates seem to go up in the area where the suicide occurred.

Cluster suicides, however, represent a fraction of the overall number of suicides, and it's impossible to tell if people are killing themselves because they're depressed or if they've been influenced by other suicides. And some experts theorize that suicides are more frequent in towns with a highly transient population (such as Pierre, South Dakota, which also has no psychiatric center within three hours' drive), perhaps because people feel rootless or less connected and more alienated.

Why Now?

In the year 2001, suicide remains the number three killer

of young people in America. Professor Thomas Joiner has a theory: In the past, he says, the American work ethic meant young people were taught that if they worked hard, they would get ahead. Their toil and effort would be rewarded. This, Joiner points out, was the overriding viewpoint throughout the 1950s, 1960s, and 1970s. These days, however, the work ethic no longer holds true.

"More and more," Joiner says, "either teens get whatever they want no matter what they do, or they don't get anything no matter what they do." He's talking about the vast class differences between wealthy and poor teenagers. Well-off teens will likely get promoted from grade to grade and accepted to college even with little or no effort on their part. If they lag behind, their parents will arrange for tutors and other specialized training to get them back on track. In contrast, even very driven and hardworking impoverished teens have a much higher dropout rate. An impoverished teen simply may not be able to gather the financial, academic, and emotional resources with which to apply to college.

"When there is a feeling of 'My behavior doesn't matter, what I do doesn't matter,'" Joiner explains, "people tend to get depressed."

Another reason teen suicide rates are rising right now is that for many teens the pressure valve has been turned way up in the last decade. Schools are more competitive. There are more demands on teenagers' time than ever before, hence the introduction of the phrase "overscheduled student." Compared with generations past, teens today have harder classes, more people to hang out with, and more places to be with them. They've got more hobbies (from extreme skateboarding to surfing the Net), more technology, more time spent dating and having sex, more time spent taking care of the house while parents are working, and more requirements for getting into college. And with twenty-four-year-old Internet millionaires appearing by the dozen, many high school teens feel they have to plot their future success starting this very instant or else miss the boat.

"Few parents can appreciate your work," writes a fourteen-year-old girl. "It takes me an average of three hours to finish my homework, plus another two to study for the multiple tests I have every day. I've repeatedly fallen asleep at my desk without finishing my work, and my mother expects me to get the same kind of scores as I used to and as my sister gets, even though she has easier classes because she's still in grade school! I can get straight As and one 89, but it still isn't good enough for my mother. And I can't stand it. The stress is so high, I cry myself to sleep at night. I almost considered suicide after I got almost all Bs on a report card. And it pisses me off."

While there are more pressures on teens than before to succeed academically and socially, there are fewer rules telling teenagers how they are supposed to act. Alternative has gone mainstream, and it is as normal at age eighteen to have a Web start-up as to have started a family or to have enlisted in the army. Such freedom can bring stress as well, and as parents are less and less involved in teens' choices, that stress increases until it can be too much to bear. Teens are making big decisions about sex, college, careers, without always having the knowledge needed to make them wisely—and the stakes are higher than ever.

Adults have years of experience to help them put things in perspective. But for teens, the fishbowl feeling that comes with being in high school means that seemingly minor events can seem like colossal failures. And, of course, some teens do experience major trauma: A class is failed, a parent dies, a girlfriend is pregnant. These are all the kinds of factors that may trigger suicide. For example, an adult woman who doesn't want to be pregnant can, in most states, legally get an abortion. But if a sixteen-year-old finds herself pregnant, she often has limited options: She may fear her boyfriend's and her family's reaction, have no access to an abortion clinic, or not be allowed, by law, to have an abortion without telling a parent. She worries about being scorned in school, being kicked out of activities, being shunned by her friends, giving up her social life, and disappointing her parents. For her, the only way out may seem to be ending her life. That's a dramatic example, but it shows how distressed teens may see their choices as limited—and sometimes they're right. That may be a reason that teenagers are the only group for whom suicides are on the rise.

By the same token, teen suicides are frequently more impulsive, with fewer warning signs, than adults'. Teens react quickly and passionately to incidents (fights, breakups, failures) and are more apt to choose suicide than adults, who have more highly developed coping skills. In the news recently there have been accounts of teens, even children, killing themselves after a mild scolding or a failed test. Teens who are expected by their families to do well are actually more likely to attempt suicide than burned-out teens with no rules at home. That's why it's up to all of us to watch for teens who are on the edge: It may be the ones who seem the most with it who need help.

What Are the Signs?

Most people who are depressed do not commit suicide, but enough do that it's worth knowing the symptoms of depression so you can recognize them in yourself and others (see Teens with Depression earlier in this chapter). But if one of your friends or someone in your family seems depressed, yet not suicidal, it's still key to get that person help. Being depressed is an arduous, joyless way to live. Depression that's untreated could go away on its own (or go away and recur in cycles), but it could just as easily get worse and worse until the person becomes suicidal.

"I have had my thoughts, and mental scarring from them," writes an eighteen-year-old guy. "The wanting to die, to just end it all, and get rid of all this pain. The need to purify myself from the hell that I went through. For a time I thought suicide was a way out, a way to end it all, and finally reach peace. But I was wrong—it was just an escape from reality and caused more harm than good. I have faced suicide through having friends, people I love and cherish, kill themselves. That hurts. It tore me to pieces when my friend of fifteen years did it. Dealing with it is no easy task, and it takes time."

In some cases, a teen commits suicide seemingly totally out of the blue. But when people look back, they can often see clues that the teenager was in trouble and at risk for suicide. Maybe he started giving things away, or quit play practice, or just seemed bummed all the time. Unfortunately, some clues become evident to us only in retrospect, after we've already lost a friend, or a brother or sister. That's why it's important to learn about suicide and about the symptoms of depression now, so that if a friend or a sibling or even an acquaintance of yours seems suicidal, you'll know to encourage that person to get help.

Isabella, 13 · Lubbock, TX

Isabella is a shy girl who has an easier time making friends online than in real life. She also likes drawing, reading, cartoons, and academics. She's close with her father, not so much with her mom, and feels like an outcast at school.

I've been depressed. To the point of wanting to commit suicide. It's awful. Every day you just want to die, for all the pain to stop, forever. I've noticed that it's a pattern. In the summer I'm fine. I'm happy. Wouldn't ever think of suicide. But then school comes, and all the people are there, and they talk behind each other's backs. How do you know that they're not saying mean things about you? Calling the kids they don't like gay and fags and inside you're dying because you know you're different. Because you don't think that that guy down the street is hot, you think one of your female friends is cute. Because you don't listen to 'N Sync or Eminem, you like Robert E. Keen and Don McLean. Because no matter how damn hard you try to not fail your classes, your grades are never good enough.

The reason for teen suicide is mostly pressure.

Pressure to be something they're not, to be society's little vision of perfection. Pressure to make the best grades possible so your mother can post a little "My kid is an Honor Student at _____" bumper sticker on her car.

My school is nice. I like most of the people. They're nice; they just don't know me. And they offend me and hurt me without knowing it. And because I take four high school pre-AP classes and am just barely managing to pass, while my parents want 95s or above, I did consider suicide. But I didn't go through with it. Because I was too afraid. And I didn't want to hurt my dad. I think it would be hard to tell if someone was depressed or something like that, because in reality, happiness is the easiest thing I've seen to fake.

How Can We Stop It?

Maybe your friend makes suicidal-sounding statements and you're afraid to tell his parents or a teacher because you think he might get mad at you. Or you're worried that he's not really suicidal, and you'll feel stupid if you say something. Or maybe he's just been withdrawing, and you can't even get him to talk about the weather, much less the possibility that there's something serious going on inside. Perhaps he's come to you for help but doesn't feel comfortable talking to a counselor or following any of the other advice you give him. All you know is that your friend's in trouble—so what do you do now?

- ***Talk to your friend.*** Contrary to popular belief, say suicide experts, you will not be giving someone ideas they didn't already have if you bring up suicide. If you suspect someone you care about is contemplating taking his or her own life, trust your instincts and say something. Just be sure to do so in a straightforward manner: Don't dare your friend to go through with suicide, as that may be the final thing that will push him to do it. If someone is truly intent on taking his own life, there may be nothing you can do or say to talk him out of it. By bringing it up, though, and encouraging your friend to seek professional guidance (a guidance counselor or local hot line can refer you to an adolescent psychologist or psychiatrist), you can feel assured you've done all you can.
- ***Listen carefully.*** A study of youths at the residential center BoysTown concluded that teens who mention suicide two or fewer times are likely to use more lethal methods to attempt it than their peers who mention suicide more than two times before attempting it. "So you really have to pay attention that first time they mention suicide," says Michael Handwerk, a BoysTown psychologist and one of the authors of the study.
- ***Involve an adult.*** The truth is that teens may be most likely to confide in a friend (as opposed to a parent or a sibling) if they are thinking about suicide. The people they are least likely to confide in, according to Dr. David Shaffer, "are their parents. They're going through a phase of life in which they don't want their parents to invade their private life too much," he adds. Which makes sense—there are probably a lot of secrets that teenagers keep from their

parents. Even very involved, attentive parents may miss what's going on with their kid. A recent Ball State University and New York State Psychiatric Institute study examined accounts of fifty-two teens who were hospitalized after suicide attempts. Fifty-seven percent of the teens said they were depressed, but only 13 percent of the teenagers' parents thought their teenager was depressed.

The scary thing about this is that if a friend tells you he's suicidal, you may very well be the only person who knows. It's vital that you act on the information, even at the risk of alienating your friend. Better to have an intact friend and a broken promise than an intact promise and a dead friend.

"I saved two of my friends' lives by snitching," says a fifteen-year-old girl. "They got mad initially, but afterward they were thankful. Many girls choose slower methods to commit suicide because they don't really want to die. It's the cry for attention. People can very much be serious about it, but I think people want to be stopped; they want to know they are loved, and if someone doesn't show it to them, well, they go and kill themselves, because what's worse than being lonely? I know that mostly people want you to say that you love them, but sometimes not even love is enough and you need to get your friend help before she leaves your life permanently. Love is having the strength to betray her trust."

At BoysTown, Handwerk says, residents are taught to report every single mention of suicide to an adult as if it were a life-and-death matter—which it is. "You have to make a distinction," he adds, "between tattling and saving someone's life."

- ***Don't make it easy.*** "About two thirds of these kids

have easy access to firearms," says Alan Berman of the American Association of Suicidology. While you can't get rid of every gun, Berman adds, if more were stored safely (separately from the ammunition and with properly working gun locks), a lot of suicides would be avoided.

- **Be on the lookout for clues.** "It's the rare kid who suicides who hasn't left a path of clues," says Berman. "Yet oftentimes, the parents will say, 'I didn't see a thing.'" What kinds of clues do teenagers leave? Some kids give away prized possessions, believing they "don't need material objects" anymore. They may threaten suicide, saying things like "It would be better if I were just dead" or "You'd be better off if I were never born." Other teens show the classic signs of depression: weeping, changes in sleep or eating habits, and a sense of hopelessness (see a more complete list of symptoms on pages 59–60). An insidious clue is when a teen who had been depressed suddenly seems to cheer up for no apparent reason. The real reason for this newfound good mood could be the teenager's belief that he has found the answer to all his problems: suicide.

Sophie, 17 · Chelsea, MA

Sophie is a private-school girl with a plaid uniform to prove it. She's trying to quit smoking so she can rejoin the track team, has friends in various cliques, and looks forward to going to college at a big university. Her parents are religious, but Sophie doesn't consider herself too into any one thing—be it religion, cliques, or school.

I had a friend who committed suicide. Late at night, he drove his truck into a dead-end street, with no houses. . . . Have you ever seen the movie *The Client*? He took a hose from one end of the muffler and put the other end to the window, just like in that movie, and he just kind of fell asleep and died. This was three years ago.

I was about fourteen. He was seventeen. We were friends through my brother. He'd come over to the house, and I had a big crush on him. He was like this really, really nice guy and you never would have guessed that this would have happened.

He was a wicked, wicked sweetie. His name was Jackie. When I was younger, I was a little bit awkward-looking—I had buck teeth before I had braces, and I was always kind of worried about how I looked, and we didn't have a lot of money so I kind of dressed like funky-weird. He'd always tell me, "Oh, don't worry about it, you're beautiful, you don't have to change a thing." He was just that kind of person, a real sweetie.

I came home one day, and my mom was just sitting there. She looked really upset. She said, "It's Jackie. Something happened to him." And I was like, "What? Did he get in a car accident?" ('Cause he had just gotten a car.) And she was like, "Well, he committed suicide." I got really mad—I didn't believe her. I was like, "Why are you lying?" When my brother came home looking like he'd been crying, I knew it was true.

We went to the wake and the funeral. It was really hard. It was open casket. Seeing your friend who was always nice and always had something nice to say, seeing him lying there, is a hard thing to go through. Everyone went to the funeral, the whole town. My brother was crying; he had sunglasses on.

Jackie didn't leave a note, but just before he died he gave away a bunch of T-shirts, and he offered his friends his old stereo. He offered me his fish. I had a big fish tank with only one fish in it. He said, "I have this little shark fish if you want it." Then he stopped coming around as much. He started getting into trouble with drinking and the police. He was getting arrested and in trouble with his parents. It went downhill from there.

Now that I look back, there were things that led up to it, but when it actually happened, I just couldn't believe it. It didn't make sense.

My brother will not talk about it. My mom tried to help me understand. She said sometimes bad things happen to good people and that you just have to understand things like this can happen in life—you can lose a friend suddenly, so you have to cherish your friendships and try to watch out for people. My dad has a very different opinion. His opinion is: "Forget about it; he's in hell." My parents are divorced, and he's the wanna-be religious type.

Jackie was too good a person; he just made a bad mistake. Unless you were a major in suicide, you'd never expect it: He was so nice you'd think it was just part of his personality to give his things away.

If you're worried about a friend, talk to him. Does he show some (or even just a few) of the signs of depression? If he does, tell him you're concerned about him because you've read about depression and it seems like he might be showing some symptoms. Tell him exactly what he's been doing or saying that has you worried (that way he can't just brush off your comments or laugh off your concern).

Don't be put off if your friend says he's fine or tries to change the subject or blow you off. If he won't talk to you about what's going on, you should talk out your concerns with someone who will listen, whether it's a trusted relative or older friend or even a guidance counselor (guidance counselors and teachers are trained to deal with this kind of thing).

Your friend might try to convince you that he is trying to "snap out of it." Even if your friend is very strong-willed, don't buy it: Depression can come and go in cycles, but the cycles are not based on how hard the depressed person tries to get better. They are based on the random patterns of the illness or the effectiveness of treatment your friend is getting. Someone who is clinically depressed or suicidal cannot will himself to cheer up or cut it out. Even though he might think that's possible, it's not. More likely, though, the person will say that everything's fine, he's just been in a weird mood lately, and it's not worth worrying about. If your gut tells you this isn't the case—trust yourself.

It's really hard to speak up about suicide, because your friend might be denying that there's a problem, or he could even get mad at you for spilling his secret if you tell his family that you're concerned. You might even find it hard to find someone to listen to you: Lots of times even wise parents will deny that there's a problem, especially if the problem could mean their kid needs counseling or other treatment.

If you feel you have no one you can talk to who will be helpful, try calling a hot line number (look for one in your local yellow pages under "crisis centers") and talk with one of the counselors. They have been trained to answer questions like this and help people get treatment they need. The bottom line is: Sometimes people really don't want to be helped, and there's nothing you can do to change that. But if you talk to your friend and consult an adult or a hot line, at least you'll know you've done all you could.

In 1994, Mike Emme, a well-liked seventeen-year-old Westminster, Colorado, teenager, climbed into the front seat of his treasured yellow Mustang and shot himself in the head. At the wake and the funeral, friends of Mike's asked his parents if there was anything they could do. "Don't do this; don't attempt suicide," Mike's parents said. "If you are ever at the point of despair, please ask for help." Those words were written on yellow cards with ribbons attached and handed out to teenagers. The idea is that it's hard to say the words "I feel suicidal" or "I need help," so instead, all a teenager has to do is hand someone he loves his yellow card, so they know he's in pain and he needs help. So far, more than fifteen hundred teenagers have obtained the cards. For more information on this project, which continues to be supported and run by Mike's parents, check out www.yellowribbon.org.

"I'm your average teenage rebel, but the only rebel-type thing I do is speed, for which I've been ticketed twice," writes a seventeen-year-old guy. "I have also thought about suicide, but have since decided against it and am working on improving my life, grades, relationship with my girlfriend, and my parents as well. My parents care for me very much. I have it pretty good—friends who are caring, a girlfriend, access to the Internet, and a whole lot of similar stuff."

There are many other organizations, hot lines (both local and national), and Web sites aimed at helping teenagers who are depressed or suicidal. (Search on Yahoo for "teen suicide" to find one near you, or look in the yellow pages under "crisis centers.") In addition, prompted by Dr. Shaffer's study with the American Foundation for Suicide Prevention, some schools have begun conducting a brief suicide-probability screening, which will help teachers identify teens who are at risk for suicide. If you or someone you care about is in trouble, please reach out. There's always a better way for a depressed person to handle her problems, but she may need you to help her see what those options are.

Teen Suicides

July 2001 · Harlan, Iowa

Eighteen-year-old Nicholas Klindt shoots and kills himself, just months after another boy, Jason Thrasher, seventeen, shot himself to death. In this town of 5,148, four other young people recently attempted suicide, reports the *Des Moines Register*.

October 1999 · Westford, Massachusetts

High school senior Todd Eager parks his Camaro in a parking lot outside an ice cream parlor and detonates a homemade bomb, resulting in his death. A few weeks earlier his teacher had posted an essay he wrote in his English class. In it, he described how happy he was with his car, his life, and his future prospects. The police chief of his town of eighteen thousand is quoted in the *Boston Globe* as saying that Todd "may have appeared normal on the outside, but he was troubled on the inside."

May 1999 · Bronx, New York

Fourteen-year-old Anna Perez uses a clothesline to hang herself to death in a bathroom stall of Herbert H. Lehman High School. The *Daily News* reports that Anna had been having trouble at home, had lagging grades, and had just broken up with her boyfriend. A few weeks prior to her death, she had been suspended for drinking alcohol in school.

SCARY STATS

Our nation's child suicide rate is twice as high as the rest of the industrialized world, .55 out of every 100,000 versus .27 out of every 100,000. If firearm-related suicides are disregarded, however, the rates become almost equal.

CENTERS FOR DISEASE CONTROL

Four causes account for 72 percent of all deaths among young people aged five to twenty-four: motor vehicle accidents (30 percent), other unintentional injuries (12 percent), homicide (19 percent), and suicide (11 percent).

1993 SOUTH CAROLINA YOUTH RISK BEHAVIOR SURVEY

Fifteen percent of people with major depression and 10 to 15 percent of those with bipolar disorder (manic depression, in which their moods swing wildly because of a chemical imbalance) will die of suicide.

DIAGNOSTIC AND STATISTICAL MANUAL OF MENTAL DISORDERS

A 1990 study concluded that parents of suicidal adolescents were more depressed, drank more alcohol, had lower self-esteem, were more anxious, and had more suicidal fantasies than parents of nonsuicidal adolescents.

JOURNAL OF ADOLESCENCE

A 1989 U.S. Dept. of Health and Human Services study found that lesbian and gay youth are two to three times more likely to attempt suicide than other youth and account for roughly 30 percent of all teen suicides. In a 1997 Youth Risk Behavior study among Massachusetts high school students, 46 percent of the gay, lesbian, and bisexual students said they had attempted suicide within the past year, compared with 8.8 percent of all students.

The CDC recently reported that the 1994 nationwide suicide rate among ten- to fourteen-year-olds has increased 120 percent since 1980—the biggest jump of any age group.

January 1999 · North Richland, Texas

High school student Randall James locks himself in a Richland High School bathroom stall in Texas and shoots himself with a 9-millimeter handgun. Classmates tell local reporters Randall was teased mercilessly, often to the point of tears.

January 1999 · Carrolton, Georgia

Jeff Miller, seventeen, and Andrea Garrett, fifteen, shoot themselves in a bathroom in the science hall of Central High School. They had been dating and left a note indicating that their death was the result of a suicide pact. Fellow students report that Andrea's parents thought Jeff was too old for her.

December 1997 · Pierre, South Dakota

Fifteen-year-old Kenny White shoots himself to death in his home using his father's pistol. He leaves a note asking his parents to remarry and his mom to quit smoking. The note also serves as Kenny's will; he indicates that he wants his friend Steven to have his baseball cards and sports equipment, and another friend, Jason, to have all his CDs.

April 1997 · Ormond Beach, Florida

Osceola Elementary School fourth grader Aaron Albright, ten, is found by his mom hanging by a rope around his neck from a tree in his Riverside Drive backyard. The coroner's office rules Aaron's death a suicide, but his family protests, saying his death was an accident. (It's common for the families of suicides to insist this, sometimes because they consider it a personal failure to have had a suicide in the family.)

The assistant principal of Aaron's school describes him as a kid with a wonderful personality who was always smiling. The *Orlando Sentinel* reports that Aaron's mom told police Aaron was upset that day because she couldn't leave work in time to take him to a Daytona Beach Cubs baseball game.

The American Academy of Child and Adolescent Psychiatry puts suicide as the third leading cause of death for fifteen- to twenty-four-year-olds.

More U.S. teens die by suicide than by any natural cause, according to the American Foundation for Suicide Prevention—about five thousand a year.

According to the CDC, the suicide rate among blacks ages ten to nineteen more than doubled between 1980 and 1995. For black males fifteen to nineteen, the rate of suicide was up 146 percent.

In 1995, the American Association of Suicidology reports, one young American committed suicide every two hours.

A 1997 CDC Youth Risk Behavior Survey revealed that 21 percent of high school students had considered suicide in the past twelve months, and 8 percent had attempted suicide within the past year.

66 Often, violent individuals are abused or neglected as children, and even more often, a means of expressing that violence (guns, knives, lighters) is made accessible to them. Parents aren't solely to blame, but they are grossly irresponsible if they do not react to warning signs displayed in childhood.

No happy, functional, mentally healthy person would ever do such harm to another human being or even to themselves. You cannot place the blame solely on the individual. Mental instability isn't a chosen trait, after all. It's learned, inherited, provoked, and fed. Every human being has some sort of darker side, but not all of us are unstable. We who are stable are not taught violence. Our parents were never violent, nor were our grandparents. We are not hurt and humiliated into hatred every day. And no one encourages us to hurt another. We are stable, functional, happy, and mentally healthy individuals. Others, however, are not, and will likely never be. One does not choose to be mentally ill."

—Chris, 19

Chapter 3
Illegal Desires:
Teen Sexual Offenders

Child molesters, even teenage ones, don't wear badges that identify them as such. Take nineteen-year-old JC, for example. He doesn't sound like a psycho, like a creep, like what even in prison is called "the most evil of all criminals." It's a little bit surprising that JC's voice is broken-deep, like that of a guy who just emerged from boyhood. JC is talking from a phone in a residential treatment center, where he's about to graduate from a sexual offender treatment program. His treatment providers say he's been a model patient, an example of how a juvenile sexual offender can be treated through a comprehensive program and become a productive member of society.

His story: He was baby-sitting for friends of his parents who had two little girls, one in fifth grade and one in second grade. They were in the bath, and one of them asked JC to bring in another towel, which he did. He then proceeded to "help bathe them" by touching them sexually. Once you've gotten away with the forbidden, it's easy to do it again, and to believe that somehow you'll never get caught. "After that," JC says, "I felt that since I could touch them there while bathing them, I could touch them there . . . other times." JC says this a tad defensively, like a kid who gets caught eating brownies that are intended "for company" and then blames his mom for leaving the brownies out in the first place.

Another time, a baby-sitter who was watching JC's younger sisters brought her own daughter over to JC's house. "I walked in on her when she was in the bathroom," JC says. "I was helping her with her clothes—and then I was all of a sudden touching her."

JC is a sexual offender, but he's still a regular teenager in a lot of ways. He's into *Star Trek* and electronic music— he's got the CDs of all the *Star Trek* movie music ("and some of the more popular episodes"). He's proud of his close-cropped haircut that marks him as an ROTC student and says he wears, you know, normal clothes. He says the ROTC is kind of like the juvenile sex offender program he's in now. In both, JC says, "you have to learn how to control yourself." He speaks cautiously, in measured words, punctuated with pauses rather than *like*'s or *um*'s or *you know*'s. When JC first molested a child, he was fourteen years old.

JC is speaking from the office of his psychiatrist, Dr. Mark Chaffin. When Chaffin is in the room, JC takes on an authoritative, teaching voice, as if he's talking to a young student come to study the ways of this species called juvenile sexual offender. When Dr. Chaffin leaves the room, JC talks more softly, and faster—like he's excited to confide the details of his story.

"I kind of switched back and forth between cliques," JC says. His words echo those of so many other teens who state that yes, their school is filled with cliques, but no, they don't belong to any one group. They say they are able to float between cliques—able to make lots of different kinds of friends. Sometimes the kids who say this are those who find themselves on the fringe of several groups, never quite accepted. They can rationalize that they have friends from all walks of life, but rarely do they have strong ties to other kids, or someone they can call a best friend. JC describes his hometown in Oklahoma as a place where kids have either "an extremely large amount of money, and you fit in with the rich people, or you have a lower amount of money, and you fit in with the lower crowd."

When the talk turns to the reason he was sent to the treatment program, JC starts pausing more frequently— long, painful pauses that seem to go on for minutes. More than once he needs prompting: "JC . . . Are you still there?" As if there had been no break, JC picks up where he left off. He gets pretty good grades and has a few friends at school, but none of them know about "what I did." JC often refers to "what I did," by which he means that he sexually assaulted children who were in his care. "You don't want the whole world to know about this," JC says. When he does tell people, "it's really on a need-to-know basis."

He also describes it as "embarrassing." It might seem to make sense that guys who sexually assault or rape would be somehow proud of it. After all, even if they were caught, they got what they wanted. But JC says that's not the case. He's in a terribly embarrassing situation, he says. He's talking not about being labeled a child molester, but about being caught and having to endlessly replay the details of his crime and his criminal thoughts to an eager audience of doctors and other patients in the treatment center. And then there are the people outside the treatment center who know about JC's past. JC rattles off the list of people he and his parents felt needed to know "what I did," for both safety and personal reasons: the pastors at his church, the youth minister, "certain family members," and the assistant principal at his school.

JC recounts the details of his crimes like he's calling a ball game—it's a story he's clearly told many times before. How can he speak so casually about something so heinous? In fact, most juvenile sexual offenders lack empathy and are unaware that they're actually doing harm to their victims by molesting them. It sounds incredible, but it explains why many sexual offenders repeat the behavior until they are caught. When, through therapy and treatment, juvenile sexual offenders come to understand the damage they have done, many of them stop molesting permanently.

It was the kids JC was baby-sitting who eventually busted him. One night during dinner, the kids told their parents what was going on whenever JC came over to baby-sit. "It didn't bother them," JC insists. "That's why they just talked about it openly the way they did." The girls' parents contacted JC's parents and agreed not to press charges if JC promised to get help, which was how JC landed in the juvenile sexual offender program in Tulsa, where he has spent the last eighteen months learning how to reprogram his thoughts, control his urges, and stop molesting.

When Sam Manzie, a fifteen-year-old in New Jersey,

molested and killed an eleven-year-old boy selling candy bars for a fund-raiser, the case turned the country's attention to the growing problem of juvenile sexual offenders. Sam, a kid who was later diagnosed with depression psychosis, abducted, molested, and killed his victim, then stuffed him in a closet and took him out to the woods later that night to hide his body. During sentencing, Judge Peter Giovine talked of Sam's consistently aggressive behavior: bringing a knife to kindergarten; torturing his family's cats and dog; even setting fire to his room. Sam got a seventy year sentence.

But the more common tales of juvenile sexual offenders aren't nearly so dramatic. It's a boy who touches his younger sister. (Is he just curious, or engaging in what could be the start of a lifetime of sexual offenses?) It's a group of guys who have sex with a drunk girl at a party. (Were they all just having fun with a willing party girl, or are they felonious rapists?) It's a teenager who kisses the nine-year-old she baby-sits. (Is she just mimicking what she saw on TV or exploiting the child sexually?) There are also more clear-cut cases of kids who fondle and rape other kids. There's a raging debate about just what behavior qualifies a kid as a juvenile sexual offender and what should be done about these kids.

There's an important difference between guys who molest younger children and guys who attack their peers or older women. Guys who attack peers tend to be more aggressive and get into other kinds of trouble as well. Their behavior is an expression of domination and control, whether it's a boy who forces his girlfriend to have sex with him because he feels it's her duty or one who attacks a girl at a party and later claims she was "asking for it."

What's Going On with Guys Who Attack Their Peers?

"I'd classify him as a little James Dean type of kid," says Dan Juengel, attorney for seventeen-year-old Michael Skaggs. "He was the bad-boy type that all the girls wanted to go out with. He's cute: He's got dark hair and he's physically fit. All the girls were interested in Michael Skaggs." Everyone knows a guy like Michael; there's one in every school—the edgy, daring boy who gets girls even though he never seems to treat them very nicely. Girls just feel special being around him because he's popular and bad, in a sexy-seeming way.

A fourteen-year-old girl told a Missouri newspaper reporter she remembers having had ten shots of tequila when Michael and two other guys invited her into a car. She was about to find out just how dark Michael's dark side was. According to her, the boys pulled the car into a dead-end section of Interstate 70 in Missouri, then Chad Lindsey, seventeen, held her down while Michael raped her. The third guy fondled her. Next, Chad too raped her.

But it wasn't just this event that landed Michael in the news. A sixteen-year-old girl claimed Michael raped her in a friend's apartment. She said he pulled one pant leg down and pushed her underpants to the side, holding her arms over her head while forcing himself on her.

Another sixteen-year-old girl claimed that Michael raped her in the basement of her house when she was fourteen while her stepfather, mother, and younger brother were upstairs. She said they had been playing pool and Nintendo before he pushed her on a bed, pulled her pants down, held her arms above her head, and forced her to have sex with him.

The list goes on. A seventeen-year-old girl claimed that when she was fifteen, Michael raped her in the men's bathroom in a park. She said Michael grabbed her arm and tried to pull her into the bathroom, but she broke free. Then he carried her into the bathroom. She said he threw her on the floor, then said not to tell anyone or he would kill her, and he proceeded to rape her.

On May 5, 1998, Michael Skaggs, of St. Charles County in O'Fallon, Missouri, was charged with raping five teenage girls in separate incidents spanning the previous two years. He was labeled a "juvenile sexual predator" (the first ever in St. Charles County) by the prosecution and held in lieu of $500,000 bail. Chad Lindsey pleaded guilty and testified against Michael. A local newspaper reported the incidents and hinted that Michael might be guilty of even more crimes—the paper urged more victims to come forward.

Michael pleaded guilty and received a five-year probation sentence from Circuit Judge Ellsworth Cundiff, who also suggested to Michael that he not show his face in St. Charles County again (Michael's family moved shortly thereafter). If Michael violates his probation, he will get seven years in prison for each of the five counts.

One reason that guys sexually attack girls their own age is "the group made me do it" theory. It goes like this: Everyone does things in groups that they would never do on their own.

Very few twelve-year-olds just decide one day to grab a pack of cigarettes and light up in the yard because they're wondering what will happen. The same goes for drinking beer—the vast majority of experimentation happens because "everyone's doing it," so it must be, if not a good idea, at least not dangerous. This mentality isn't always a bad thing; sometimes groups can pressure each other to do good things too. Examples are study groups that help their members get better grades or groups that volunteer in hospitals or senior citizens' homes.

But a group mentality can be dangerous, too. Sometimes groups feel invincible, and a group can take on an energy that its individual members could never conjure on their own. For example, on October 10, 2000, four River Rouge, Michigan, high school football players (all aged sixteen and seventeen) were arrested and charged with criminal sexual conduct. They had allegedly forced a fourteen-year-old cheerleader into one of their homes and then raped her. As in many other gang-rape cases, these guys had reacted to pressure from their pals to be cool, to join in the score, with nightmarish consequences for everyone involved.

If you are in a group setting that starts to take a dangerous turn (you know the feeling you get in your gut when this happens), you should ask yourself: Would I act this way if I were alone? Do I want to get involved in this? Can I stand up for myself and this potential victim by getting help or getting her out of here? We are all responsible for our actions and for the safety of those around us, even if we are not directly involved in harming anyone. Doing nothing to help is the same as being part of the problem.

But not all sexual assault between peers occurs in groups. Acquaintance rape happens when a guy forces his girlfriend or a girl he knows to have sex against her will. (And unfortunately, it's not rare: As many as three quarters of all rapes are committed by someone the girl or woman knows.) In a majority of these cases, one or both of the people involved is drunk: One study found that 55 percent of female students and 75 percent of male students involved in an acquaintance rape had been drinking or using drugs at the time. These cases often go unreported (as few as 5 percent are taken to the authorities), either because the girls feel too embarrassed or too concerned about their reputation to speak up, or they feel no one will believe them if they do. Since these cases are usually built on he-said she-said testimony, they can be difficult to win.

The dangerous thing about drinking is that it clouds the judgment of everyone involved. So a girl who would never otherwise even consider kissing a guy might find herself, a few drinks later, going further than she wanted to. And once a guy is all revved up, drunk himself, and raring to go, it can be very difficult (if not impossible) to get him to change directions and stop, even if the girl is clear that she no longer wants to have sex. "I've had nights when I would be out drinking or getting high," says a fifteen-year-old girl. "I've had no clue where I was, alone in a park or puking in a public bathroom. I have come very close to being raped while I was passed out. I'm lucky that my close friend was there at the time to stop it from happening."

In a situation like this, is the guy a violent rapist, or is he simply a hormonal boyfriend who used too much pressure and ended up talking his drunk date into something she didn't want to do? The fact that it's extremely difficult to recall what happened when you're drunk just complicates things even more.

According to the journal *Pediatrics*, girls aged twelve to nineteen are victims of rape or sexual assault more often than any other age group. Don't up your odds of this happening to you or someone you care about: Don't drink and date. It's not just unwise; it's unsafe.

The other way girls can give off mixed signals without meaning to is by agreeing to fool around to a certain point and then pulling back at the last minute. While this is completely within a girl's right to do, as a practice, it depends on the boy being able to calm himself down enough to respect the girl's wishes. The sad fact is, some guys, especially guys like Skaggs who obviously have a power trip going on, might not care to put on the brakes.

And then there are guys who have somehow gotten the idea that having sex with a girl is more about conquest than about love. These guys may feel sex is owed to them in return for a date or just because they desire it. That's why it's important for a girl to go on group dates or to public places until she's sure the guy she's with can be trusted.

Daniel, 16 · Ventura, CA
Daniel goes to a public high school that has a
McDonald's across the street. Now that he's a junior,
he can leave campus during lunch and head for the
golden arches. He says his school is based on cliques:

*the surfers, the gang-bangers, the guys who stage
WWF- style contests in their backyards, the potheads
. . . the list goes on and on.*

Date rape? I surround myself with people who would not be in that situation. If you hang with the right people and you don't drink or do drugs, you're not going to know people who experience it. Drinking mostly is how it happens. But I have heard of it because I'm not deaf.

The one situation I'm thinking of was traumatic to the girl but not horrible. When you're a girl, it's hard to talk to a guy who's looking for sex because he's going to try to press you, which is something I know because, well, I'm a guy.

The instance I'm thinking of, she was a sophomore and the guy was a senior. She was at a dance, and before the dance she'd had too much to drink. I don't know how she got into the dance because they have a Breathalyzer at the door. They have to. If they didn't, everyone would just be drunk for every dance.

Then the couple went off and left the dance—the girl's older sister knew the guy and told her get away from him, avoid him. I mean, the guy was nineteen. He'd been held back a few times. But he had a nice car and I guess she was thinking he was cool and I guess they went off somewhere. They came back a few hours later, and she was crying hysterically. But what I don't understand is this: After it happened, she actually started dating the guy again.

*   *   *

The interesting thing about Michael Skaggs' horrible raping spree is that in several of the cases, the girls hung out with Michael and his friends after the rapes took place. Michael's attorney used this in his defense, saying that Michael didn't actually rape the girls. Michael claimed that yes, he had sex with them and then didn't call them, but his crime was essentially that he was a bad boyfriend, not a rapist.

This was a theme repeated by lots of kids, that the guys would attack a girl and then the girl would keep going out with him. Why? Probably because girls are socialized to prize their boyfriended status or they feel they're in love, perhaps for the first time. So they fall into the guy's dangerous cycle: He'll abuse, then apologize, then abuse again.

Andy, 17 · Houston, TX
Andy goes to a "normal public high school," by which he means his classes are overcrowded (he's got thirty-eight students in his English class) and sometimes it's physically difficult to walk down the hall because of all the kids. He's a trumpet player in his school concert band, and he's in marching band. Most of Andy's friends are band guys too. His school is economically and ethnically diverse, which Andy thinks is great. Andy really wants to be a rock star— in addition to school band, he plays bass with other kids in an as-yet-unnamed punk band. His influences? Led Zeppelin, and his favorite band of all time, Red Hot Chili Peppers. Though he describes the kids in his school as very fashion-conscious, Andy sticks to

T-shirts and jeans and his one vanity item: thick-rimmed, black rectangular glasses.

There's a lot of dating at my school. Some people, they'll date for a week and then there are some people who've been dating for years. It seems like there's a lot of sex. I don't really know much about it though. I know there's a lot of people who drink a lot and I guess that's fine if that's what they want to do, as long as they don't mess with me.

I'm dating a girl right now. She goes to a different school. And she has spiky hair—she's a punk-rock chick. She's really, really intelligent, she's fifth in her class, she's a senior and I'm a junior. I met her at a show: FYP, Diesel Boy, and Teen Idols were playing. She has a good sense of humor—she's really fun to be around. We go to shows a lot.

Friday night she came over and we had spaghetti. I made the sauce from scratch. I've only been dating her for like a month. We see each other like once a weekend. We just really get along well. We're not having sex right now. I'm not against that by any means: If two people want to do that, I guess, why not, as long as they're safe about it. It's not like a priority for me, I don't really think about it that much. I guess if it happened I'd just be like, Okay, it happened. I wouldn't feel bad about it or regret it or anything.

I don't understand date rape. That's so empty to me. It's pretty sad. If your priority in life is to have sex, I think you have a pretty sad life. I don't get the whole date-rape thing. I'm sure people do that, but I don't think I would really enjoy it unless the other person was enjoying it. But some people are kind of messed up. There's a lot of messed-up people.

I know a lot of kids who aren't innocent. Kids do crazy stuff. Just like some of these stories I hear on Mondays, like, "Oh yeah, Friday night I was so drunk I was driving around and I don't even remember what happened . . . but it was awesome! Tomorrow night I'm going to go do the same thing again!" But since the guy's a kid, people assume he doesn't know any better—or that he's a victim of the evil alcohol ads or something. Date rape is sort of the same kind of thing. I guess it's human nature to have sex. Some people are just more forceful about it—which is really sad. I wouldn't even be able to comprehend being able to do that—I'm really empathetic toward the feelings of others. Anyway, I bet people blame pornography for this kind of thing. It's not pornography's fault, it's the kids' fault! Kids are just as horny as anyone else.

What's Going On with Teenagers Who Molest Children?

In contrast with smooth-talking guys who may attack peers, guys who molest younger kids (who make up the majority of teens charged with sexual offenses) tend to be socially maladapted. Most have few ties with family and friends and have a hard time with normal social activities like meeting people and making new friends. Why they assault children depends on how they grew up, their mental state, and what they get out of the experience. Just as no two crimes are alike, no two offenders have the same reasons for what they do. Experts have identified some reasons why a teenager might sexually assault children.

Theory #1: They're Curious Everyone goes through a phase of sexual experimentation—sneaking peeks at porn, making out, or asking friends detailed questions about sexcapades that may or may not have actually taken place. Teens who are very socially awkward may feel more comfortable with little kids than with kids their own age (not that this is in any way an excuse for their behavior, but it may explain it). A shy guy who's feeling really turned on but doesn't have an outlet for his sexual energy may decide to molest kids out of curiosity.

One of the reasons some adolescents molest younger children is "because they can," says Dr. Mark Chaffin, JC's doctor, who is also associate professor and director of research at the University of Oklahoma Health Sciences Center on Abuse and Neglect. "Children are relatively easy and available outlets for adolescent interests."

As JC puts it, "With sex, it's like you hear a lot about it but you haven't experienced it—maybe you're not ready for it, so you try this. Then you like it really well and end up doing it over and over and it gets out of control."

Theory #2: They've Been Abused Themselves Sometimes a guy who is accused of pedophilia—having sex with or sexually fondling kids—was himself a victim of child sexual abuse. You might think: If he was molested, wouldn't he know how horrible it was and wouldn't he do anything to avoid inflicting that kind of pain on others? That's true to an extent, because most kids who are sexually abused do not go on to become abusers themselves. But, explains Phil Tedeschi, clinical supervisor and founder of a program called the Sexual Offender Resource Center in Denver, Colorado, "What is not uncommon is to see a profile that we call victim-to-victimizer."

He explains the theory like this: "When a young person is violated—in any way, but let's say sexually—he feels that somebody has taken his power away. Because the power was taken through sexual assault, he may see an opportunity to regain power through assault of someone more vulnerable than himself. If you add sexual excitement to that moment of feeling powerful, it is a process that can become habitual. For a young person who walks around most days not feeling powerful, those are very seductive emotions. They like it, and they repeat the process." In this way, Tedeschi explains, sexual offending becomes addictive, so that even if the teen wants to stop or knows what he's doing is wrong, he may feel unable to quit.

Another explanation that supports the victim-to-victimizer theory is that memories of being sexually abused can become sexual fantasies for those abused kids once they get older. Gail Ryan, who has studied juvenile sexual offenders for almost twenty years and is author of the book *Juvenile Sexual Offenders*, says it's not because the kids liked the abuse in any way. Because the teen's first sexual experience was of being abused, it "can become the source of sexual arousal—these kids will reenact their own experiences."

"To the best of our knowledge," says Tedeschi, "I think we would say about fifty percent of these offenders have been sexually abused. If we broaden the definition of sexual abuse to abuse in general, including physical, emotional, and neglect, we're looking at almost a hundred percent."

Though a recent University of Michigan survey concluded that 72 percent of children who sexually abuse other kids were abused by adults when they were children, other studies put the number at closer to 40 percent.

"At first we thought the number one risk factor was being abused themselves," says Gail Ryan, "even though we knew that most people who are abused do not go on to become perps. Research has found that children who are physically abused and neglected become sex abusers even more than kids who have been sexually abused."

For kids who are physically or emotionally abused, sexual assault is about trying to get a feeling of dominance, a feeling of control, and they somehow come up with the idea to sexually abuse other younger kids to gain that power and control. Where does that idea come from? Sexually explicit TV shows? Friends or relatives? Researchers still aren't sure.

So can experts who treat juvenile sexual offenders always look back into the guy's past and find the incident or incidents (physical abuse, emotional abuse, sexual abuse, or neglect) that caused him to sexually abuse others? "There are a few cases where we have a problem determining what the cause is," says Tedeschi, "but often that just means it's really hidden."

Theory #3: They're Out-of-Control Control Freaks JC has met a lot of other teenagers who are in treatment for sex offenses. "Some of them," he confides, "I'm not saying this about myself, but some of them kind of doctor up their story a little bit to make it sound more like they did it deliberately, to make it sound more like they're in control."

Gail Ryan says sexual abuse happens when a progression of thoughts, feelings, and behaviors in the abuser are triggered by a stressful situation—one in which he feels totally out of control. It's usually something that reminds him of an earlier life experience. Sexually molesting somebody else makes the guy feel better, more powerful, better able to handle the stressful situation because now he's gained control over something.

"They act out sexually to reduce anger or anxiety or to gain control, or to make others feel as badly as they do," Ryan says. Making a littler kid feel powerless helps the molester feel very in control, powerful, and excited, which is perhaps a feeling he longs for but rarely experiences outside of this situation. In addition, there's the pattern that goes along with any sexual encounter: excitement, mounting tension, followed by sexual release. This makes the guy feel good . . . so he repeats the cycle.

What makes these kids feel so out of control in the first place? It can be lots of things: not fitting in at school, feeling alienated, feeling ignored at home or disconnected from the community. It's important to know that different people will react to similar situations differently, so that what one teenager perceives as a horrible home life might be perfectly tolerable to someone who is less sensitive or more able to roll with the punches.

For JC it was his family situation that made him feel out of control—two disabled younger sisters at home needed most of his mom's attention. His grandmother, who lived with them, was very ill. His father was often absent. (JC says he models himself on his father and considers himself a workaholic. He also says he never wants to get married or have kids. Why not? "I don't want to subject them to the lack of family closeness we had," he says.)

"I can't tell you exactly why I did it," JC says. "I can tell you there was a lot of stress and there was this . . . feeling . . . that I couldn't take care of by myself. It wasn't necessarily a sex thing. I just did it one day, and it made me feel better. It didn't hurt the other person. It just made me feel better."

Theory #4: They Lack Empathy JC's ignorance of the harm he caused to his young victims is common in juvenile sex offenders, says Gail Ryan. In a *Journal of Interpersonal Violence* article, she states, "Youthful offenders appear at one extreme to be unaware of the seriousness of their behavior and at the other are very aware and uncomfortable with the deviance. Very few, though, have any sense of the abusive aspect." It seems impossible that someone could hurt a child and not realize he was doing so—especially since child sexual abuse is so repellent to most people. How could someone like JC not know he was causing harm to the kids he baby-sat for by fondling them? Is he just in denial?

Not necessarily, says Ryan. The more likely cause is what she calls an attachment disorder—which means the offender is incapable of bonding with other people in a normal way. Combine that, Ryan says, with the lack of ability to feel empathy, which she often sees in young sexual offenders, and you've got a guy who really doesn't know how to feel someone else's pain.

You know how when you see a sad movie you cry for the main character? Well, people who don't feel empathy would just watch the movie with dry eyes and wonder why everyone else in the audience seems so upset.

Ryan thinks that this mind-set stems from being neglected or being cared for in an inconsistent way when the guy was a baby. Look at it this way: If sometimes a baby's cry brings love and food, but other times crying brings hostility or neglect, that baby is going to be confused—he's programmed to cry when he needs something, but the crying isn't getting him what he wants. He feels helpless, not cared for, and unloved. Since he himself is not cared for in an empathic way, he does not learn how to be empathic.

In contrast, Ryan says, babies who are consistently well cared for begin to show signs of empathy as early as eighteen months. A lack of empathy, combined with communication and accountability issues (for example, the abuser tells himself his victim wanted the abuse or incorrectly assumes that he didn't harm his victim) are two traits that Ryan thinks all juvenile sexual offenders share. These traits must be addressed—before they become too deeply ingrained—in order to effectively treat sex offenders.

Who's Doing This?

When imagining a child molester, most people conjure up an idea of a perverted older man who hides in the shadows and pounces on his young prey. In fact, a vast number of child molesters are boys who play Little League during the day, then climb into bed with their younger brothers for an advanced game of doctor while Mom and Dad are sleeping. They are baby-sitters who get straight As, take their young charges to G-rated movies, then fondle these children in the name of bathing or dressing them. They are stepbrothers who "teach" their little sisters how to kiss or have sex, or eighteen-year-old guys who toss off their tuxes to force sex on their passed-out, underage prom dates.

Juvenile sexual offenders are 90 to 95 percent male. You might think you'd be able to pick out a kid like JC a mile away, but, sadly, that's not true. Mark Chaffin, who's one of the nation's leading experts in juvenile sexual offender research, says that all kinds of kids pass through the center where he treats juvenile sexual offenders: brains, jocks, popular kids, and outcasts. "We see kids who are highly delinquent, who make poor decisions in most areas of their lives," Chaffin says. "We also see kids who are very popular, well-mannered, polite, and get good grades—they run the gamut."

In other words, it could be anyone. "These kids are similar to kids you know," says Tedeschi. They also have a specific personality type: It's kind of scary, but one thing most of them have in common is that they're really charming. "They're very manipulative; they're capable of snowing people. These are the kids who are in your schools, churches, malls, who are hired as baby-sitters, or put in positions of trust with siblings or cousins."

You also can't pick out a kid based on his shady past.

A National Adolescent Perpetration Network sample of 1,600 juveniles who molested children found that while 30 percent had three or more nonsexual offenses on record and there were a few who were failing school, the majority did average or better in school, and had no other police record.

So is there any way to predict who will engage in sexual-offender behavior? These guys have some characteristics in common, and researchers are hoping that by studying kids who are at risk and those who have offended, they can get better at predicting and preventing acts of child molestation. Here are some traits that juvenile sexual offenders tend to have in common:

Their Families Are Often Messed Up A large number of these kids have a parent who's died or abandoned the family, and lots of them have spent time in foster care or other out-of-home placements. A majority experience addiction, domestic violence, or physical abuse at home. Judith Becker, a major pioneer in the field of juvenile sexual offenders, analyzed twenty years' worth of studies about juvenile sexual offenders. Her research indicates that most youth sexual offenders come from middle- and lower-income families. She also discovered that many have parents who are cold and unaffectionate. At the other end of the spectrum, sometimes they have parents who give them too much information about sex (for example, Dad keeps *Playboy* lying around, or their parents engage in sexual activity within eye- or earshot of the kids).

They May Be Wired Differently When something terrible

happens, we often try to find reasons why the unfortunate person's situation is different from our own. If a girl gets mugged on her way to school, we might say, Well, she was going to school at seven A.M. and I usually go at seven fifteen, when it's lighter out, so that couldn't possibly happen to me. It's natural to want to distance yourself from terrible things. In the same vein, researchers at first assumed that juvenile sexual offenders had some kind of biological defect that accounted for their behavior. On a biological level, the theory went, these people are different from the rest of us.

To explain this theory further: A person who is aroused by something that's considered not normal is said to have a paraphilia. A paraphilic can be someone who gets turned on by looking at pictures of people being hurt, someone who exposes himself in public, anyone whose sexual tastes lie outside the mainstream. So, the thinking went, maybe teenagers who get sexual with children are just hardwired to be aroused by kids (the word for that is "pedophilia"). But it turns out that's probably not the case.

"Initially," Gail Ryan says, "we assumed that the majority of these kids would have deviant arousal patterns. But the research has been clear that most of the kids have normative sexual interests," which means juvenile sexual offenders get turned on by exactly the same things their peers are aroused by. In other words, they're scarily normal.

"Sometimes, though," says Mark Chaffin, "you can see a young man who is beginning to develop a sexual interest pattern in children, and there are some suggestions that biological factors might be involved. We've got kids in treatment here who have been very high-functioning in every other area of their lives except this one. We even have athletes and honor society kids. Why they end up pursuing this behavior is not something that they understand; it's not something that we understand very well."

Why Now?

There are currently eight hundred treatment centers for juvenile sexual offenders (JSOs) in the United States and three hundred for JSOs under the age of ten, thirty times as many as ten years ago. Why would there be such an enormous growth in this subpopulation? There are several theories (of course!).

There Is More Pornography Now On the whole, if there's one message to take away from the JSO experts, it's: Parents, hide your porn! "Parents are careless and leave this stuff lying around, especially high-level porn—the triple-X-rated, very graphic stuff. Almost eighty percent of juvenile sexual offenders have been exposed to this prior to offending," says Phil Tedeschi.

Interestingly, JC doesn't think it's porn's fault that there are more juvenile sexual offenders now than ever before. "I don't know what I was thinking," JC says, "but I've never been exposed to pornography or anything like that." But most juveniles who sexually offend *have* been exposed to pornography, says Tedeschi, who does blame the higher incidence of juvenile sexual offenders today on readily available porn.

Gail Ryan also feels that greater exposure to sexual stimuli at a young age has contributed to the rise in juvenile sexual offenders. She blames not just porn, but also the sexual messages kids pick up from TV shows, magazines, even kids' games.

There Are More Blended Families Now Chaffin says that in addition to the increase of access to porn and the mixed messages about sexuality present in magazines, on TV, and in video games, there is a higher percentage of stepfamilies now than in past years. "Abuse occurs more often between non-blood relatives," he says.

Tedeschi agrees. "Abuse occurs at the hands of stepparents [and stepsiblings] much more often than at the hands of biological parents."

We Now Know What to Call It As recently as a few decades ago, no one wanted to believe child sexual abuse happened, so when a little girl complained that her older brother was fondling her, she might get shushed or even punished for making up lies. These days, as a society, we are more sophisticated about sexual abuse and more alert to the signs. This means we can more easily identify the perpetrators and get them into treatment, whereas previously they might have gone unrecognized until adulthood, or even forever.

Even today, though, "a lot of times it gets swept underneath the rug," says Dr. Jacqueline Paige, clinical director for the University of Tennessee at Memphis Adolescent Sex Offender Program (ASOP). "It's sexually assaultive when a thirteen- or fourteen-year-old is fondling a younger sister or brother, and a lot of times that gets dismissed by parents. Maybe every kid doesn't need residential treatment, but if you have a thirteen-year-old fondling younger children, that's sex-offender behavior," she says.

Finally, there's also the possibility that it's not the amount of sexual abuse that's increasing but the frequency with which it's reported. Perhaps in our more open-minded society, victims feel less afraid of coming forward, and increased sensitivity in law enforcement means that parents and children can feel more assured that complaints will be taken seriously.

What Are the Signs?

It's harder than you might think to identify a teenager who might sexually abuse a child. "You can't tell who's going to do it," says JC. "Everyone in the program, we all say, you couldn't tell that we would have done it just by looking at us." JC knows what he'd look for if a guy was hanging out with his little sisters, though—the types of guys he'd want to protect them from.

"I'm watching for too pushy, too much touching, too soon into a relationship," says JC. "Getting too intimate too quickly, and if someone does a large amount of sexual talking, that's someone you have to worry about. If they're that open in public, how open are they in private?"

There are some other characteristics that should make you wary. Oftentimes before a sexual offender strikes, he'll check out potential victims to see if they'll go along with his plan quietly or put up a fight. Sometimes he'll start off, say, roughhousing with kids and "accidentally" brushing up against or grabbing their genitals. Be concerned if you witness this kind of behavior, because this could be the preliminary to more invasive behaviors. Horseplay, crossing boundaries, playing doctor or house . . . sadly, it *sounds* like pretty normal stuff. The key thing to remember is, if something makes you feel uncomfortable, follow your instincts. You're probably right.

"Look out for kids who might engage in extremely controlling or intimidating behaviors," warns Tedeschi. "Be suspicious of unusual generosity, especially if it's used to establish control."

Other signals? "Be careful about a young man or boy who is constantly trying to get a young child or children alone," says Chaffin. "Or someone who is being overly erotic in his behavior with young children, encouraging secrecy with a child. And be particularly careful about a young man who seems to be much more interested in interacting with young children than with kids his own age."

So should you be suspicious of every teenager who wants to play with kids? No, says Chaffin. "The good news is, as near as we can tell, this is relatively rare behavior."

How Can We Stop It?

You can go to www.apbnews.com, click on your state, and find out whether you've got a sex offender living in your area. This is a result of New Jersey's Megan's Law, which requires that communities be able to find out about sexual predators living nearby. (The law was named after a girl who was raped, then murdered by a recently released sexual offender who had moved in across the street from her.) For the most part, this law is a good thing. People in a community rightly feel entitled to know if they have a convicted pedophile living next door to, say, a day care center. But for some adolescent sex offenders, the law may be overzealous.

Take the case of Jason Nester, a sixteen-year-old boy whose parents moved to the small town of Fordland, Missouri, in October 1998. The family had chosen Missouri because there was no law requiring juvenile sex offenders to register in that state—when Nester was nine, he'd served three years in a detention center for raping a younger boy. However, a few weeks after they settled in, an anonymous fax about Jason's past arrived at the police department in Fordland. Word spread around the town of five hundred quickly, and the family was nearly ousted. Slowly, tolerance set in, but Jason is still being home-schooled, and members of his family still fear for their safety.

As a result of incidents like this, some judges have removed juvenile sex offenders' names from the national sex offender registry on a case-by-case basis so that once they've been treated, they can become functioning members of society and not pariahs.

Dr. Mark Chaffin says the boys who pass through his eighteen-month residential program have only a 7 percent recidivism rate. Still, he says, "we have to notify neighborhoods of their presence because they're 'dangerous.'" Chaffin adds, "to call a twelve-year-old who touched his sister twice a pedophile is probably an overreaction." Referring to the old "You're imagining it" philosophy of child abuse, he says, "We've gone from collective denial to a sort of collective overreaction."

This is also the case with the current trend toward trying juveniles as adults. It's a particularly bad idea to do this with juvenile sex offenders. Juvenile centers are aimed at rehabilitating and treating, whereas adult prisons are meant primarily to punish. The movement toward punishing children as fiercely as adults has been termed by those who treat juvenile sexual offenders "the war on children." This applies to the case of Sam Manzie, a boy who was let down by the system at every turn.

As a young teen, Manzie got involved with a forty-two-year-old pedophile over the Internet. Authorities found out and made Sam a reluctant participant in their sting operation against the man. Sam became depressed and even hinted at wanting to hurt a child. His parents begged the courts for help, begged them to put him in a psychiatric facility, but to no avail. As punishment for molesting and killing a ten-year-old boy, Manzie was sentenced to spend seventy years in lockdown twenty-three hours a day. The adult who molested him was convicted of two minor charges.

Manzie's case was one of clear-cut abuse, but some experimentation that goes on between young children is considered normal. The first task of the authorities in a case of suspected abuse is to establish that what happened was really abuse and not mere sex play or exploration between two kids.

Gail Ryan, facilitator of the National Task Force on Juvenile Sexual Offending, defines abuse as an incident in which there is coercion (one person persuading or cajoling the other person to do something), lack of equality (one kid is much older and/or much smarter than the other), and lack of consent (one kid forcing the other kid to be sexual with him).

"From what I've read, there are high cases of repeat offenders among sexual offenders," says a nineteen-year-old. "If you're sixteen or seventeen, you know what's wrong, and being younger than an adult doesn't change the effect of your crime in any way whatsoever. If the kid is smart, he should get therapy. But if he's not going to get better, the goal should be to just keep him in the system and process him as an adult."

Once a juvenile sex offender is identified, treatment usually lasts at least a year and is well suited to a residential (live-in) program. The teens being treated live in dorms, attend intense daily therapy sessions (individual, group, family, offense-specific, and so on), and take classes. The parents also need to be treated with counseling. ("Some of the parents of kids in here just abandon them," JC says. "It's sad.")

And so begins the long, slow, pricey task of teaching these boys about healthy sexuality. Tedeschi calls it cognitive restructuring, which basically means teaching them to think in a whole new way. "We have to create a new process where the client will think, feel, and behave differently. We figure out what those thoughts are [that trigger the molesting behavior], how they drive the abusive process, and then we try to establish the opportunity for new truths to form. And with those truths, new emotions and alternative behaviors." First the offender is helped to understand why he abuses and what situations or triggers make him abuse, then he is taught to deal with his emotions in a more healthy and positive way.

Christopher J. Alexander, a psychologist in Santa Fe,

New Mexico, describes the seven basic tenets of treating sex offenders that he and many other juvenile sexual offender treatment providers follow:

- *Individual therapy* identifies their unique problems, and *group therapy* provides counseling with others so that offenders learn they're not alone in their feelings and struggles.
- *Sex education* is provided so offenders can learn the details of anatomy.
- *Social skills training* teaches offenders how to interact with others in a healthy way. Alexander emphasizes that the number one goal for sex offenders is to teach them "how to be laughed at by others without falling apart." They need to understand that being out of control is part of life and not something that must be reacted to with sexual violence. The boys also must be taught empathy, so they understand that their actions affect other people in both positive and negative ways.
- *Anger management* helps them convert their emotions into acceptable behaviors, such as punching a pillow or creating art. The offenders are also taught healthy ways to deal with anger they may have as a result of their own abuse and neglect.
- *Relapse prevention* helps offenders accept their desires without acting upon them.
- *Substance abuse treatment* is given to the many offenders whose abuse of drugs or alcohol clouds their judgment or gives them courage to offend.
- *Aftercare* must be available so that therapy and help are

accessible to the person after the program officially ends.

There haven't been studies done on adolescent sex offenders who receive no treatment, but these teenagers, according to Judith Becker, likely fall into three categories: those who do it and then stop, those who commit more sex crimes as well as other crimes, and those who continue to molest and develop a paraphilic arousal pattern (in other words, they become addicted to the molesting behavior). It's this last one that's the doozy—because each pedophile can abuse hundreds of victims. As Chaffin put it, "There are tons of victims, but a few men out there are doing a whole lot of molesting."

About 20 percent of all sexual offenses are committed by adolescents, according to the Association for the Treatment of Sexual Abusers. For the victim, the trauma is no less intense than what she would suffer if an adult molested her. Further, 60 percent of adult male sex offenders say they started sexually abusing kids while they themselves were adolescents. Given that each juvenile sex offender has multiple victims—and if not caught, JSOs usually grow up to become adult sex offenders, who are much harder to treat and can victimize hundreds over a lifetime—it is vital to catch juvenile sexual offenders and get them treatment as early as possible.

The good news is, "juveniles are very plastic," says Alexandra Phipps, Ph.D., a psychologist at Atlanta's Highland Institute who has worked extensively with sex offenders. "They're still growing and their identity is still forming." This makes adolescents very treatable, but it can also result in a paradox: "You would want to be very careful about labeling a boy a sex offender for life because he could still do a lot of changing," says Phipps. "On the other hand, you do want them to be held responsible for their behavior because adolescents tend to get away with a lot." For this reason, the National Adolescent Perpetrator Network refers to juvenile sexual offenders as Sexually Abusive Youth—thereby labeling the behavior, not the juvenile himself.

"Almost always the parents are the bigger problem," continues Phipps. "They minimize what the kids have done. There is so much excuse-making. I had one kid who confronted his mother during a group and said, 'Mom, I did it! I did it! Quit defending me, it's not helping me.' Most important, you have to address it early on. We wait way too long. We need to believe that children can be perpetrators of sexual offenses. I've had nine-year-old clients who put their penises in three-year-old little girls' bottoms."

But even JC, a "reformed" juvenile sex offender who will soon be released from his center, shows some confusion about his treatment and his overall views of sexuality: "I myself was never extremely open about sexuality in public or private," he says. "Then I end up doing these sexual acts in private and I get caught and I learn that you can't do these sexual things in private or public but you have to be willing to talk about sexuality in private and public."

Gail Ryan emphasizes that "we need to teach everybody how to define what's abusive and to know that it's not okay to be abusive. We need to be telling kids about the laws. They don't know that they'll be arrested at ten or eleven or twelve for doing something sexual." She warns, "Don't keep secrets. Secrecy allows a lot of things to continue."

Most important, says Ryan, adults spend a lot of energy teaching kids how to recognize dangerous strangers or "bad touches," but perhaps not enough time teaching teens how to act safely with others. The lesson, she stresses, isn't just about how to identify evil in others, but how to see it in ourselves. "We need to tell kids how to keep themselves safe," says Ryan, "and how to *be* safe with others."

Sexually Violent Teens

July 2001 · Palmdale, California
A thirteen-year-old boy (whose name was withheld from the press) is charged with sexually assaulting a seven-year-old girl. The girl required surgery to treat her injuries.

June 2001 · Denver, Colorado
A fifteen-year-old boy is accused of molesting a nine-year-old boy repeatedly over the course of a year. The alleged victim and attacker lived near each other, and their parents arranged frequent visits.

October 2000 · River Rouge, Michigan
Four high school football players (all aged sixteen and seventeen) are arrested and charged with criminal sexual conduct. They allegedly forced a fourteen-year-old cheerleader to one of their homes and then raped her. One of the boys' attorneys calls it "an unfortunate incident."

July 1999 · Little Havana, Florida
A fifteen-year-old student is charged with the violent rape of

a five-year-old girl. The teen fails three polygraph tests before confessing. The alleged rapist was a friend of the girl's sixteen-year-old brother. The boy says he raped the girl in her home on July 24. According to the *Sun-Sentinel*, the ordeal lasted hours and had the victim running from room to room, trying to escape. The little girl was slammed face-first into a wall so hard that a tooth was knocked out. She was hospitalized with internal injuries.

October 1998 · Chicago, Illinois

Arnold Roberts, sixteen, becomes the first juvenile offender from Du Page County to be charged as an adult. He is accused of sexually assaulting a series of women who ranged in age from twenty-three to sixty-two. His string of assaults allegedly began when he was fourteen. He pleaded guilty to charges stemming from four of the attacks and was sentenced in March 2001 to fifteen years in prison.

September 1997 · Jackson, New Jersey

Fifteen-year-old Samuel Manzie is

SCARY STATS

Texas reported 541 young sex crime offenders in 1998, more than double what it was in 1995.

Juvenile sex offenders (age sixteen or younger) in Illinois accounted for 17 percent of the total number of criminal sexual assault arrests in 1995.

THE ILLINOIS CRIMINAL JUSTICE
INFORMATION AUTHORITY

Reports to police and social services about incest, lewd conduct, and even rape come once a day to Palm Beach County, Florida, agencies, according to the *Sun-Sentinel*. Police report that some perps are as young as five or six.

70 percent of children who sexually abuse kids have at least one parent who is drug- or alcohol-addicted.

THE JOURNAL OF CHILD MALTREATMENT

arrested and charged with the molestation and murder of an eleven-year-old boy. The boy had been participating in a school fund-raiser, selling candy and gift wrap door-to-door, when he was abducted, molested, and strangled to death.

November 1996 · New Orleans, Louisiana
Six teens are arrested and charged with gang-raping a fifteen-year-old female classmate in a vacant class-room at their high school. Two teen-agers, ages eighteen and seventeen, are named in the local papers; the other suspects' names were kept pri-vate because of their age.

March 1993 · Glen Ridge, New Jersey
Teens Kyle Scherzer, Chris Archer, and Kevin Scherzer lure a fifteen-year-old mentally retarded girl into a basement. They gang-rape her, then violate her using a baseball bat and a broomstick.

According to the FBI, from 1988 to 1992, the number of juvenile arrests for forcible rape increased by 17 percent, while similar adult arrests increased by only 3 percent.

"Some people say that teen pregnancy isn't anyone's fault except the girl who decided to jump in the sack, but I beg to differ. It takes two people for a teen pregnancy to happen. The guy makes half the decision, and the girl makes half the decision. A lot of times it does come down to the girl having the final say, but that certainly doesn't make her decision more important than the decision of the guy. They've both made a decision—who cares who decided first?

There's also the issue of birth control, which both parties should also be thinking of. If a girl doesn't want to go on the Pill or something, that doesn't mean that she's asking to get pregnant. Guys can use birth control too. Sex should be an equal decision between two people, but sometimes it seems like everything is up to the girls. We are aware of what could happen, which makes us usually less eager to have sex than guys. Girls are pressured into doing it, often before they are ready, and may not feel completely confident about their decision. But if something happens and a girl gets pregnant, the fault is hers? I guess I just don't see the logic behind that."

—Ricki, 16

Chapter 4

Dangerous Sex:
Teen-Adult Affairs

In 1995 GLENN HARRIS, a thirty-three-year-old Manhattan gym teacher, and his fifteen-year-old student/girlfriend, Christina Rosado, were featured in newspapers nationwide for weeks on end. Harris, who later claimed that the girl's parents were abusing her (these claims were never proven) and he was helping her escape, took off with Rosado for an eight-week cross-country tour. When he was finally caught, he was charged with kidnapping. He pleaded guilty to a charge of custodial interference and was sentenced to three years of probation.

In November 2000, sixty-two-year-old math tutor and special-education teacher Paul Kerner was sentenced to thirty-three months in jail for having sex with a sixteen-year-old student. Kerner brought the Sheepshead High School student to Atlantic City, New Jersey, where he videotaped her wearing a swimsuit and talked her into engaging in oral sex. The student, whose name was withheld in the papers, testified in court that she had been previously sexually abused and forced into prostitution by her parents when she was thirteen. It was revealed in court that Kerner knew about her tragic past before he molested her.

What's Going On When Teen Girls Hook Up with Adult Men?

Girls hooking up with older guys is a trend that's surprisingly accepted in America. Think Woody Allen and Soon-Yi Previn. (Soon-Yi was twenty-one when her adoptive mother, Mia Farrow, found proof that she was involved with the fifty-six-year-old Allen, whom Farrow had been with for years.) Or Jerry Seinfeld and Shoshanna Lonstein. (They started going out when he was thirty-eight and she was seventeen.)

"We have teens dating adults every day in this country," says Marilyn Anderson, director of education for Planned Parenthood in southwest and central Florida. Anderson is currently one of two hundred Planned Parenthood educators teaching a curriculum called Unequal Partners, which was developed in 1997, to address this very concern. "For the most part, as long as it's a heterosexual relationship," Anderson adds, "society is very supportive of it."

A nineteen-year-old guy knows what Anderson means. "When I was in high school, I knew this girl who was doing something with one of her teachers," he says. "She transferred over from another school—it was rumored that she had to because she was going out with one of her teachers there. After a while we saw her hanging around (and practically on) one of the teachers a lot. They were together during breaks, after school . . . I even saw them getting into the same car a few times. And her dad didn't seem to mind, even though he was a teacher too. After graduation, there was an announcement in the paper about the engagement of the girl to her teacher."

Dating an adult when you're a teenager can make you feel very in control and powerful, which is ironic since more often than not it's the adult who has power and is abusing it. Unfortunately, girls who get together with older men are commonly misperceived as seductresses who conned the guy into engaging in a sexual relationship.

The truth is, teenage girls often do want to date older guys—any teenage girl (and many a frustrated teenage guy) will tell you that. That hot camp counselor when she's a counselor-in-training, the teacher's aide who's just a few years older, the guy who delivers the papers in his beat-up (but still cool) car are all potential crush targets.

It's natural as a teenager to want to be seen as sexy, as flirty, as capable of having an adult relationship. The problem is that it's easy to get caught up in looking and acting more adult than you really are, like lying about your age to get into clubs or dressing in a sexy way because it feels good to get attention. Supersexy clothes send a message—"I'm an adult, I'm ready for sex"—but the girl sending the message may not be ready for the reaction she's bound to get. Some of these girls end up in bed with much older guys, or simply in risky sex situations, the kind that lead to pregnancy, disease, and (not least of all) crushed self-esteem.

In today's society, it doesn't even seem so weird to see, say, a sixteen-year-old girl dating a twenty-two-year-old guy. But the fact is, it's against the law, and with good reason: The difference in their ages makes the nature of the relationship unequal. Why? Because the older partner has more life experience and (usually) more sexual experience. The older partner has the freedom to make his or her own choices, while the younger partner is still the responsibility of her parents. The younger partner is more naïve: the older partner can promise the world, and the younger partner isn't sophisticated enough to know whether he means it. The older partner can pressure the younger partner by telling her what's normal, since she doesn't really know what's true in the adult world. That's why, in most states, a minor cannot legally consent to sex (which means even if a fifteen-year-old girl wants to have sex with her twenty-year-old boyfriend, he can still be charged with statutory rape).

So is a May-December relationship a social problem or just a personal choice? Lawmakers hedge on where to draw the line; parents and teens often differ on what's okay; police rarely enforce statutory rape ordinances; and as for the couple, well, the social scorn often just makes them feel even more destined to be together.

The thing is, no matter how a teen girl looks or acts, no adult should use flirtatiousness or burgeoning sexuality as an excuse for taking advantage of her. Too often, what starts off as a thrilling adventure for a girl can turn into a nightmare as the relationship progresses. Usually, girls report, once they're romantically tied to the guy, he changes. He starts making demands—for sex, time, or attention. It's not that he's necessarily a bad guy, it's just that a nineteen- or twenty-year-old has different needs than a fourteen-year-old. So while he's insisting that she be home when he calls, testify her undying love, and go all the way when he's ready, she's still young enough to be intimidated by his demands (and perhaps too insecure to stand up for herself). After all, this is a girl who's still figuring out who she is, making time for yearbook committee, and trying to pass midterms.

The worst-case scenario is painted by Michael Schulman, author of *Raising a Moral Child*. "Girls who date older guys feel they have control over nothing, except they have some control over this guy and he's got a car and money. The girl thinks 'I can control it, this guy's eating out of my hand . . .' and then a short while later, she's coming home with a black eye."

Though this may seem like a dramatic example, there are lots of reasons why dating an older guy is a bad idea for most teen girls:

Pressure to Have Sex Whether or not the girls think they're going into these types of relationships with their eyes open, the fact remains that many of them are getting into something they can't or won't know how to get out of. As a result, many of them end up having sex when they don't want to.

Child Trends, a Washington, D.C.–based nonprofit group that researches issues affecting children and teenagers, conducted a study to measure how much girls wanted their first sexual experience. Girls were asked to use a scale of 1 ("not at all wanted") to 10 ("very much wanted"). Just 10 percent of all teenage girls rated their first sexual experience a 10. "Those girls say, 'I wanted to do it, it was spontaneous, it was romantic, it was exciting,'" reports Child Trends scholar Kristen Moore. But as the age spread between the girl and the man got bigger, the "wanted-ness" of the experience went *down* for the girl.

Once the age spread was at seven years, the girls were *twice as likely* as girls who had the same age or younger partners to say their first sexual experience was involuntary. "Those girls really did feel that the guy got them drunk, or they didn't know how to say no, or they lost control of the situation," Moore says. A full 24 percent of girls age thirteen or younger at the time of first intercourse reported the experience as "unwanted sex." Other findings:

- Teens whose first partner was five or more years older were almost twice as likely to become pregnant as a teen.
- The closer in age teen girls and their partners were, the more likely they were to use contraceptives during their first sexual experience.

The Child Trends study also found that for girls who were younger than fourteen when they first had sex, only 18 percent had a partner within a year of their age. Pretty scary, right? Think about a thirteen-year-old girl you know and an eighteen-year-old guy you know. Would you feel comfortable about the two of them engaging in sex?

Teen Pregnancy There's another reason why these relationships are cause for concern. Teen girls who date older men are not only having sex before they're ready and often against their will, but they're often getting pregnant as a result.

Educators, policymakers, and teens were shocked in 1995 when the Alan Guttmacher Institute unveiled its study results showing that men over the age of twenty cause five times more births among junior-high-age girls than do junior high boys, and 2.5 times more births among high school girls than high school boys do.

Teenagers engaging in sex with adults are 20 percent less likely to use a condom than teens having sex with teens, according to the Centers for Disease Control and Prevention. It's not surprising that the Alan Guttmacher Institute found that half of the fathers of babies born to teen girls are adults. True, a percentage of those girls are eighteen and nineteen, but what's alarming is that the younger the girl is, the older the guy tends to be; the average age spread for a fourteen-year-old girl having sex is 6.5 years. In other words, there are a whole lot of fourteen-year-old girls having sex with guys aged twenty and older.

It also turns out that in a lot of cases, teen girls who have sex with adult men are doing so while under the influence of alcohol or drugs. About 20 percent of teens who get pregnant say they were intoxicated when they had sex. Drugs and alcohol (which adult men can buy legally) lower inhibitions, making it more likely that a girl will go all the way.

These guys may have bad judgment, but they aren't stupid; none of them would ever say to the girl, "By the way, if you get pregnant, I'm out of here faster than you can say 'child support.'" But sadly, that's often the case. "In high school we had a parenting group for students who had babies," says a nineteen-year-old teen mom. "I was the only one out of thirty girls who was still with the father. That's disgusting. I know those girls are having such a hard time."

Jennifer, 16 · Glendale, AZ

Jennifer was never your typical high schooler. She

enjoyed music class but was not big on academics
and spent much of her time skipping school to hang
out at her house while her parents were at work. She
left high school at fourteen and was home-schooled
for a while. She describes her school as having a
preppy student body filled with students who "didn't
give a rat's ass about anything except for partying."
But that was two years ago—now she's given up a lot
of her old ways, and her old friends have vanished
too. She's six months pregnant and just trying to save
some money before the baby comes. Jennifer lives
with her parents. She says her dad used to be
verbally abusive when he drank, but he's stopped that
behavior, and Jennifer says they're close now.

I met my boyfriend in December of last year. We
were just friends for a while. He was standing at a pay
phone outside a grocery store. I was with a couple of
my friends, and we asked him if he was old enough to
buy alcohol. He wasn't, but he said he had other stuff
and asked us to come over and smoke some weed. He
wanted my phone number. I wasn't really interested in
him, but he kept trying to get me to be with him, and
eventually things happened. He pressured me into it,
really. Looking back, I think it's probably because he
couldn't get anyone his own age.

I guess I was kind of using him. He was making
$3,500 a month. He was twenty then, and he had a lot
of money to spend on me—clothes, CDs, expensive
jewelry here and there. I never believed I was in love,
though I wished I was, especially when I found out I

was pregnant. We'd used condoms, but I don't think he put them on right, because they always broke.

He threatened me that if I had an abortion, he couldn't be responsible for what his family would do to me when they found out. He told me about all his relatives who'd been in jail or were in jail. He said he'd stick with me, though, and help raise the baby. He even took a second job, because he said he didn't want me to work while I was pregnant. Then last week, all of a sudden, he told me he didn't want to have anything to do with me or the baby, and he left. I could have been working all this time, and now I've got nothing.

Not all older guys are going to screw over their younger girlfriends. I've dated other older guys before. I think there should be laws in place, just in case they do. My parents and I couldn't press charges against my boyfriend for statutory rape because I'm over the age of consent. But we're pressing charges against him for sexual misconduct with a minor and intimidation. If I had never gotten pregnant, I wouldn't have done this, but he basically put me in this position and then he just leaves.

My parents didn't know I was sexually active, obviously. They thought these guys were real nice guys, because at first, they were. But when I was fifteen, after I'd broken up with my first boyfriend, I went out with his best friend and lost my virginity to him. That's when I started seeing a lot of different guys, and my parents didn't like a lot of them. I wasn't looking for anything serious. I don't like guys my own age and probably never will. They can't grow goatees. When I was fourteen, I was looking for a guy who could drive, could give me freedom.

My parents are going to help me out raising the baby. It's going to be a boy. They've had their share of problems, but it's clear that they really love each other, and I think that's cool. If it's possible, I want to get my GED, which I'm working on now. I really suck at math, so it'll be hard. I'd like to go to law school, maybe start at a community college and go from there. But that'll be a while. I still have a few friends who I've been close to for years, but I don't even hang out with them in a typical week.

I'm not scared of having the baby anymore. I haven't started any classes, but I see a doctor regularly. I read about it on the Web. I have lots of books, and I subscribe to all the magazines. I'm not scared about the labor. I was at first, but I'm not anymore. I just don't know what I'm going to say when he asks, "Do I have a daddy?" I just want to make sure he's happy and safe.

The other day, I heard a girl close to my own age say, "I wanna have a baby. I think I'm ready for one. Me and my boyfriend love each other. I've baby-sat and I love kids." It makes me so mad. But you can't get through to anyone by yelling, especially a teenager. I just tell them exactly what I'm going through.

I would tell a teen girl who's dating an older guy to be careful. I'm not going to tell them not to do it. I wouldn't have listened if someone told me not to do it, so I wouldn't expect anyone else to. But sexually active kids, if they're not on birth control pills, which they really should be, should always use condoms. People tell me, "Oh, it's too expensive to buy four condoms a day." That's what my boyfriend and I used— we were very active. Of course it's expensive, but no matter what, it's cheaper than an abortion or raising the child. And there are a lot of diseases out there. One friend got pregnant because she just refused to use birth control. I think she knew she'd wind up pregnant and she didn't care. I think she thought it would fix her relationship, but he left her about a week before she found out she was pregnant.

While Jennifer didn't know what she was getting herself into, some other teen girls (like the friends Jennifer talks about) seem to actually try to get pregnant. Perhaps they're seeking love or stability that's missing at home, or maybe, in their community, getting pregnant at a young age is considered the norm, as is the case with Jackie.

Jackie, 17 · Winder, GA

Merry Carol Kelly is a high school home ec teacher ("It's Merry," she introduces herself, "like Merry Christmas") in Winder, Georgia, a town where the median household income is about $32,000 and most adults are blue-collar workers. Merry can tell you in two words the biggest problem at her school: teen pregnancy. "It's like they want to get pregnant," she says. "It's practically expected of

them." Jackie was one of Merry's students. She's
engaged to a twenty-one-year-old guy.

I'm pregnant. Five months. I've been around babies
a lot: My brother just became a father, and my aunt just
had a baby. Her baby was really sick and they said he
wasn't going to make it, but he's fine—that experience
made me want to do medical work with babies. I was
going to go to college to be a registered nurse to work
with babies. I have an older brother who will be twenty
in August. His fiancée was sixteen and he was eighteen
and fixing to be nineteen when they got married.
They're divorced now. I'm still with the daddy of my
baby—we're engaged. The wedding's going to be after
I graduate. My parents love him to death.

I met him through church. We were both in the
same youth group, and some of the kids from our
youth group were dating and we just went out a couple of times. Then we got together as a couple. I was
fifteen when we met and he was nineteen. Now I'm
seventeen and he's twenty-one.

With me being so mature for my age, it just
doesn't work out when I date someone my own age.
There's really not much to talk about—boys who are
my age do the same thing as I do: go to school. With
my boyfriend, we talk about work, family, what we're
going to do when we get married. We talk about how
we're going to design our house, what colors we'll
have—I like cranberry and emerald green with light-
colored carpet or wood floors. I definitely want to have
cranberry in our kitchen—we've picked patterns out

of magazines. I want us to live near my folks. I'm looking forward to just having my own family, living out on my own, me and him supporting our kid, starting a little family. I want to have one more, but I'll wait until after school. Everyone at school is real supportive. It's not so unusual—I know at least six more pregnant girls in my grade. I'm sure there are more in the school; I just don't know them.

So, what's wrong with this picture? Jackie isn't a weepy, repentant teen who feels she's ruined her life. Rather she is a cheerful young woman who feels her life and her family are off to a brilliant start. And what's with her parents being so supportive? Jackie mentioned that yes, her parents were upset "at first." But after the initial shock and weeping, they got behind her decision to marry her boyfriend. Her mom's even helping her plan the wedding. What's the deal?

The answer is that the perception of teen pregnancy is affected by cultural differences. Jackie's mother also married her high school sweetheart and had her first child when she was not much older than Jackie is now. In a community like Winder, getting married and having children is a way for girls to get respect and be recognized as grown-up.

Child Trends scholar Kristen Moore says this attitude in a community is the result of its having reached "the tipping point." It's the same thing that happens, she explains, when a community that has been inhabited mostly by people of one race suddenly sees an influx of another race. At a critical point there will be a shift; the neighborhood will become known as one that is mostly inhabited by the newer group, and the color of the community will change.

"I think that's what we see in teenage childbearing," Moore says. "You get certain communities where it's at such a level that it becomes normative. The families are not upset about it." What we need to do, Moore and many other activists argue, is get the tipping point going in the other direction. "We need to get to a point where it's like it is in Europe, where teen pregnancy is considered something that's simply not done."

We have a long way to go: Though rates are presently dropping, the United States remains the developed nation with the highest teen pregnancy rate in the world.

What's Going On When Teen Guys Have Sex with Adult Women?

The first time Vili Fualaau met Mary Kay LeTourneau, he was in second grade. He was in her class again as a twelve-year-old sixth grader. By that time he appeared to be more man than boy: the young Samoan-American had had a growth spurt and now wore his hair in a ponytail down his back.

LeTourneau had a crush on him—even the other students could see that. There were jokes about it flying around the school. Though she was in her mid-thirties, married, and had four kids, she began a sexual affair with Vili on June 26, 1996, just before his thirteenth birthday. Both said that Vili initiated it. Then, as now, LeTourneau talked about Vili as the love of her life, her soul mate, her spiritual companion. Vili describes their union a little less romantically. "I wanted to bone her," he told a reporter. He also said he'd bet his cousin Tony $20 that he'd be able to pull it off. As LeTourneau's marriage got more and more shaky, she announced to her husband, Steve, that she was pregnant—with Vili's child.

In March 1997, a cop spied LeTourneau and Vili getting hot and heavy in a van, and LeTourneau was arrested. In November 1997, LeTourneau was charged with two counts of child rape, and Judge Linda Lau handed down a suspended sentence of seven and a half years in prison. A condition of the sentence was that LeTourneau was to have no contact with Vili. LeTourneau retained custody of her child by Vili; her husband and four other children moved to Alaska.

But LeTourneau couldn't stay away from the young man she insisted was her other half. In February 1998, LeTourneau and Vili crept out to the movies together (ironically, the flick they picked was *Wag the Dog*, in which the president stages a war to shift attention away from his affair with a minor). After the movie, they were parked and steaming up the car windows when Seattle police officer Todd Harris spied them. He ran a check on the license plate and discovered that the car belonged to LeTourneau. The officer also discovered that Mary and Vili had $6,200 in cash on them and that LeTourneau's passport was hidden under the carpeting beneath the gas pedal. Judge Lau reimposed the sentence of seven and a half years, and LeTourneau was remanded to a women's prison in Washington State.

LeTourneau's mom, Mary, was a homemaker, and her

dad, John Schmitz, was a Republican congressman for Orange County in California (his platform was his staunch opposition to sex education in public schools). But in 1982, it was discovered that Schmitz had been having an affair; he had a mistress with a fifteen-month-old son and another child (also his) on the way.

There were other rocky circumstances within LeTourneau's childhood home: accusations that she'd been sexually abused. When she was eleven and was supposed to be watching over her three-year-old brother, Philip, he fell into the pool and drowned. During her sophomore year at Arizona State University, she became pregnant and married Steve LeTourneau (a native of Anchorage, Alaska) months before their first child, Steven, was born.

And what about Vili? Rather than acting the victim, he defended their relationship to the world. The boy, his mother, and LeTourneau even wrote a book together called *Un Seul Crime, L'Amour* (or *Only One Crime, Love*). "We wanted to tell the real story of our relationship," Vili told reporters. "The bond we had, the spiritual feelings. It's unfair. I want Mary to be with me."

"It was adultery, that I don't dispute—but not a rape," Vili's mother was quoted as saying in 1998, after she had come to accept her son's relationship.

In April 2000, however, Vili and his mother filed a $1 million lawsuit against the school district, saying it failed to protect him from the teacher's sexual advances. The lawsuit said the relationship resulted in psychological damage, pain and suffering, injury to the relationship between him and his mother, and the cost of raising two children.

It's not so common that an adult woman has an affair with a teenage boy, but that's not to say it never happens: In July 1998, teacher Julie Feil, thirty-two, was sentenced to almost seven years in prison for having sex with a fifteen-year-old student. And in August 1998, Rebecca Ann Schroeder, twenty-eight, was sentenced to twelve months in jail, a year of house arrest, and five years' probation for having sex with a thirteen-year-old boy. "When a thirty-five-year-old man sleeps with a young girl, he's reviled," says Dr. Gerald Shiener, a psychiatrist and chief of consultation for psychiatry at the Detroit Medical Center. "When the woman is older, it's not exactly condoned, but it seems like less of a big deal, and people make jokes like 'I wish I had her as my sex-ed teacher.'"

A fifteen-year-old guy sees it this way: "There's the double standard thing—people say that it's okay for girls to date older guys, but it's weird when an older girl dates a younger guy. It's like the older you get as a woman, the older the guys you date are 'supposed' to be. I think when an older girl dates a younger guy it's like child molesting. This might be from my perception that girls mature faster and it's taking advantage, but that might not be true."

Who's Doing This?

Though there are rare instances of boys having sex with adult women (and the case of LeTourneau was so famous it bears mentioning in this chapter), it is far more common for teen girls to have sex with adult men. There are many reasons for this: Girls who have sex early, and those who have risky sex or sex with adults, are usually the same girls who are having a hard time with other parts of their lives, and they're looking for love and acceptance. So the challenge for experts becomes figuring out what is the cluster of factors that make it likely that a girl will engage in risky behavior.

This was the sole purpose of a major 1995 study that surveyed over ten thousand teens, asking them what made them turn to risky behavior, from smoking to not using seat belts to unprotected sex. What the researchers found wasn't too surprising: The girls who are most likely to have sex with an adult are those who have been raised in poverty. They're girls who don't have high hopes for their future, girls who may have been sexually abused or ignored or neglected, and are searching for some adult attention that they can't seem to get any other way. Teens who were more likely to engage in risky behaviors were those who had little or no connection to their school and community, and little parental involvement in their choices.

"The girls tend to have been repeatedly victimized," says LaWanda Ravoira, executive director of PACE Center for Girls in Florida. "Perhaps they have been in foster care or have been sexually abused. They almost exclusively have been without much positive parental influence. The girls may see these guys as their only family."

Dr. Gerald Shiener sees many adolescents in this situation. He says he would probably be able to go into a high school classroom and pick out the guy or girl who would be most likely to strike up a sexual relationship with an adult. "There would be two populations I would look for," he says. "First I would start out with the shiest child, the one who's a little bit aloof—that child might be more vulnerable to attention from an adult who purported to care about him or her." The second population? "A child who is pseudo-mature, a child who tends to act like a little adult. That type of behavior is often masking feelings of longing."

Besides the obvious attractions of an older guy (he has a car, more money, and more experience than a high school guy), Child Trends senior scholar Kristen Moore says, "The girls *could* be in love." Then again, Moore says, they also could be "acting out, thrill-seeking, or enjoying the power they have over this man."

It's not that these girls are unintelligent or easy prey. On the contrary, lots of them are precocious. When you're in high school and the guys in your grade are busy blowing spitwads at one another through plastic straws, a guy with a job and a car and his own apartment and cool older friends can seem very appealing. At least at first, the older guy calls when he says he will. He's much faster to say "I love you" than a younger guy. He buys you presents and takes you to dinner because he's got more disposable income than your average fourteen-year-old boy. And a girl who doesn't have a father figure in her life is even more likely to be searching out attention from an older guy, who might use the line "I'll take care of you" to get her hooked.

"When I was thirteen, a friend of mine was doing drugs, drinking, going to parties, and having relationships with eighteen- and nineteen-year-old guys," says a seven-teen-year-old girl. "I didn't like the idea then, and I still don't—thirteen is too young. She hadn't developed men-tally or physically yet, but she had lost her virginity in sixth grade. I think that is pretty sad. At that age, I don't think it's possible to understand what you're getting into. Nowadays friends of mine are having sex, but they are ready for it, and there's not all that much of an age difference between my friends and their boyfriends."

And what about the guys? Who are these men who think it's okay to seduce teenage girls? All evidence points to the fact that adults who engage in sex with teenagers are major underachievers. "They tend to be disadvantaged financially, so maybe they're not viewed as desirable partners by women their own age," says Kristen Moore. "I've heard anecdotally that they think the younger girls are less likely to have an STD. And maybe the girls are less demanding, more adoring."

It's not just any adult who approaches a teen—it's usually an adult who the teenager looks up to, like a teacher, a coach, or a parent's friend.

"Often it's someone who's in a position of authority," says Dr. Shiener. "The worst perpetrators are the teachers, the pastors, or maybe a teacher's aide, who will strike up a relationship with a young student." Shiener adds that when you talk to the teenager after the relationship is over, the first thing they often say is they were flattered by the attention. And the second? "I didn't think that a teacher's aide (or a pastor, or a coach) would do anything wrong." The obvious damage here is that the teenager can no longer trust anyone. "They get a weird idea of what authority is," adds Dr. Shiener.

This is why many teenagers, even those who think dating out of their age group is okay, say they're opposed to relationships where one person has power over the other. "If they really care about each other, if there's no inordinate pressure from one partner to stay together, then I don't see anything wrong with the relationship. But I don't think student-teacher relationships are right," says an eighteen-year-old boy. "The teacher has power over the student, whether he or she abuses it or not. So the student may be in the relationship because of the teacher's influence. And it can be difficult to tell whether they're really in love, or if one is and the other isn't, or whether the student—or teacher—is scared to get out. The teacher might be black-mailed if he or she tries to get out of it. It makes the situation much less complicated to forbid student-teacher relationships."

"I think that you'd have to wonder," Shiener continues, "all things being equal, what a nineteen-year-old and a fourteen-year-old have in common. A fourteen-year-old is still really a child, and the nineteen-year-old is an adult." No matter how mature the teenager is, or how immature the adult, the adult has the intellectual and emotional advantage, which is to say that, without exception, adults who date teenagers are taking advantage of their role, and of the teenager.

"I have a friend who's seeing an older guy," says a sixteen-year-old girl. "She is one of those girls where you're not sure if she's being used or is doing the using. The reason that I say this is because the guy is married. She's sixteen, he's mid-twenties. But that's not the worst of it. What's really bad is that she's seeing two other guys besides the married one! And she brags about it! I refuse to talk to her on this subject because I know that we will get into a fight, and that will end our friendship. We used to be really strong friends, but we drifted apart. We're barely friends now."

Matt, 18 · Cape Cod, MA

Matt just graduated from a small high school where cliques weren't as big an issue as teen pregnancy and suicide. He's worked at a youth center for two years and is starting college next month to study criminal justice so he can be a cop. He lives with his mom—his dad left when he was three and hasn't been in touch since.

Before I started high school, there was one teacher there who supposedly had sexual relationships with a few students. But I don't know if it was true. While I was there, we had one teacher who was actually stalking a student. He told her he loved her and couldn't live without her. They weren't even involved. She reported him, and he got fired.

The biggest age difference I've seen was a senior and an eighth grader. I think if you're in high school and you're dating someone who's not in high school, it's such a big maturity gap between those years. Those two kept it quiet on purpose, so not everyone knew about it. They were only together a few months. A couple of us made the guy realize it wasn't the most appropriate thing to do. He's kind of an outcast at school, so I guess when he found someone who was willing to have a relationship with him, he did it. The girl got a lot of status with her friends because here's an eighth grader going out with a senior. Now he's in a healthy relationship.

There should definitely be laws about that kind of thing. I mean, a fifteen-year-old having sex, it isn't the right thing to do. It doesn't matter if it's with a fifteen-year-old or a nineteen-year-old, it's just too young. I've seen guys do it because they just wanted to take advantage of the girl, and also because they just genuinely liked the girl. But still, they should know better. We even had one girl bring a thirty-five-year-old to the prom. It's just scary.

Last year there were a lot of incidents of date rape and that kind of thing. Most of it you hear through gossip. But a lot of them turned out to be false, and when the police would investigate, it turned out these were girls who'd been assaulted by their fathers, and they said a stranger did it so they wouldn't get in trouble. The cops would investigate—they work really hard to get that kind of thing out of our town, but you can only do so much.

My school has the second highest pregnancy rate in the state. I know a lot of girls who are pregnant, and I feel like most of the time it's with guys closer to their own age, because it's the younger guys who aren't aware of the consequences, who aren't responsible. The chairman of our school committee flips out if you mention contraception, and his two daughters are actually at risk. They just teach us abstinence, which obviously doesn't work. And they try to make kids more aware by having us carry around those mechanical kids, but most people just rip the batteries out anyway.

A few years ago, one of my friends was working at a youth center where parents who don't have anywhere else to take their kids can send them after school. I went to visit him, and I really liked it, so I started volunteering. I've always loved working around kids, so it really clicked. The first year, I was a volunteer, and I played with the kids. They hired me the next year, and I basically acted as a mentor. I was supervising, planning, trying to be not just an authority figure but also a positive role model. The kids were about fourth grade and up, Hispanic, Laotian, white, whatever, but what they had in common was they just wanted a place to hang out. They never had anyplace to go.

You can definitely see when you work with these kids that they're already starting to get certain attitudes and act certain ways because they see older kids doing it or their parents doing it. You try to help them see that just because they're in a certain situation doesn't mean they have to act a certain way. It's a long-term process, and if you find a kid who'll stay for the whole process, you're lucky.

It's hard when you get kids telling you stuff and you just don't know what to do with the information. Like you have twelve-year-old kids telling you they're sexually active. And we had limited training and resources, so I wasn't always sure what to do.

Why Now?

As mentioned above, we have become accustomed to the fact that young women frequently date older men in our society. A *Newsweek* survey showed that 45 percent of the American public thinks that if Monica Lewinsky and President Clinton had a relationship, it was her fault for pursuing him. When Bryan Peterson, twenty-four, was arrested in July 1998 on charges that he had sex with a sixteen-year-old Simi Valley, California, girl, the local paper printed this quote about the teen girl from Peterson's boss: "She may be sixteen, but she sure doesn't act like it—I believe she totally instigated everything and went way overboard."

These examples and many others show that there is still a prevailing view that if a teen girl gets involved with an older man, she is the one steering the relationship. It's an attitude that is out of tune with the reality of the matter, that girls are often taken advantage of by older men who have more power and authority than they do.

One reason this kind of relationship is happening so frequently now is that the Internet has made it faster and easier to meet all kinds of people. There are even chat groups and Web pages devoted entirely to arranging (illegal) meetings between older men and teen girls. The Internet is an anonymous place for older guys to stalk teen girls, who feel a false sense of security that comes with being nameless and faceless. She may begin sharing personal details with a guy she thinks really cares about her. He may even lie about his age to get her hooked. Then the two meet, begin an affair, and it's all downhill from there.

Ron, 19 · Alfred, NY

Ron is in his first year at Alfred College, where he hopes to study mechanical engineering. He spent a year at a small Midwestern in-state school first, trying to get his grades up. Ron's grades coming out of high school weren't great—in fact, he barely graduated. Instead, he focused on making music with his friends and hanging out with a mix of motorheads and rebels. But once he was living on his own, he became a good student and managed to get a scholarship to a better school.

Over the summer, I worked in a state-run office with a guy who was about forty. The girl he was dating was fifteen, and they'd met on the Internet. Every day he'd tell me details of what they talked about, what she was like, some personal sex stuff too. He was married, and she knew that, but he really thought it was a romance.

He's got a twelve-year-old daughter. I said to him once, "That would be like if our boss"—who was a little younger than the guy—"was dating your daughter." He just replied, "Truthfully, I wouldn't care as long as he was taking care of her." I don't know if he was in denial or what. They both just thought they were in love.

For her, I guess it's the mystique of having an older man, someone who is already in the world and has his life set up. She would get an instant life out of it. I think that might be attractive to social outcasts. In my experience, normal girls, they have a group of friends and you sort of date within that group and with people you meet through them; most girls are comfortable staying in that circle. But social outcasts are just looking for anyone who will take them.

They were talking about how as soon as she'd graduated, he'd pick her up and they'd get married. It was like an escape thing for her. She had some serious issues herself. She'd been raped, her mom was really strict, and she wasn't close to her dad. She hates her mother and wants to get away from her. She likes her dad, but he lives across the country, so she doesn't have a father figure at all, no one she can identify with. With this older guy, she can get away from her mom and get a guy back in her life. She told her older brother that she was dating this guy, and he just said, "Maybe that's too old." Her mom's strict, but she can't control the girl. This is a way she could lash out.

Basically, from what I could tell, she thought this guy was going to be her white knight on a motorcycle. It was obviously unhealthy, even if they were in love. When people over twenty or so go for teenagers, it's almost like they just want fresh meat. Sometimes they just want a playing field where they're the best available options. Younger girls will think they're cool just because they're older; girls their age might just think the guy's a loser.

I think the definition of whether or not kids should be with adults depends a lot on the circumstances. If it's a seventeen-year-old having sex with a fifteen-year-old, that's just sort of normal. If it's violent, there would need to be some sort of intervention, maybe not jail. But the charge of statutory rape can be kind of cheap. In my opinion, a lot of times it's brought by parents who are trying to live their kids' lives for them. There are circumstances where I understand it being a crime. But if it's a normal, healthy thing and the parent is making the decision "I don't like this person, so he's going to jail," that's not right.

One of my friends this summer had just graduated high school and he was dating a girl who was going to be a sophomore. Three years is about the most you can do at that age. There was a kid at college last year, he was nineteen, dating a fifteen-year-old. That's pushing it a bit much, stretching it a bit. I think if you're under twenty, two years is the most that it should be. But I don't know, they met in the same school. To say "There are people you can be friends with but you can't date who you meet at school," that probably doesn't make much sense to kids. But we still teased him about cruising by the middle school.

One of my friends got pregnant and then hooked up with this older guy after the father left her. The older guy started going around telling everyone the kid was his, even though it wasn't. The couple broke up, and for some reason, he kept saying it was his kid. Well, her mom got mad and threatened to have him arrested for statutory rape if he didn't stop telling people he was the father. She had no complaints about him while he was going out with her daughter; he only was a criminal after she got mad at him.

The biggest age difference I've ever experienced was four years. Having been an eighteen-year-old going out with a twenty-two-year-old, that didn't really make a difference. It was a little weird, just because of social stigma, but once you get to a certain level, it doesn't matter. But in high school, it's a big deal to date someone that much older or younger because of the rate you're changing at that point in your life. In a two-year time span, when you're sixteen or eighteen, your life can change drastically. It can happen when you're older too, but when you're young, you're trying to figure out who you are, and the difference is just too big.

What Are the Signs?

So when does a couple go from being okay to creepy—what's the cutoff? Someone can be classified as a pedophile if he's sixteen or older and imposing sex on someone five or more years younger than himself, says Dr. Shiener. "It's not really clear," adds Shiener. "Obviously five years is kind of arbitrary. If someone's [the victim] in a pedophiliac relationship and suddenly that person has a birthday, it doesn't instantly get normal."

Here are some questions you should ask yourself if you think you're in an unequal relationship, no matter what the age difference. They are phrased as if the person in power is a guy, but you can substitute "she" for "he" if you're a guy and ask yourself these same questions.

- *Does he promise you a better future but you never see him taking steps to get it?* For instance, does the guy talk about getting married and having kids with you, but he's already married, or he can't hold down a steady job?
- *Does he threaten you, saying if you look at other guys or see anyone else, he'll hurt you or he'll hurt himself?* This kind of emotional blackmail is not about love; it's about control.
- *Does he ever say, "If you loved me, you would do this"?* Guys who are really in love don't try to use that love to convince their partner to do something.
- *Does he ever use your age against you?* For example, does he say, "When you grow up, you'll understand why this is the way things are," or "If you were more mature, you wouldn't ask me those questions"?
- *Does he try to convince you not to use birth control or condoms to prevent pregnancy and the transmission of sexually transmitted diseases, including AIDS?* Again, this is a sign of someone who's being controlling, not loving.
- *Does he try to isolate you from your family and friends by telling you that "they just wouldn't understand" your relationship? Does he try to make you keep the relationship a secret?* A guy who claims he doesn't want to share you is actually afraid of what would happen if other people got a look at what your relationship is really like. This could also mean he's dating more than one person and wants to keep both (or all) of you in the dark about each other. Not a good sign.

If you answered yes to any of these questions, you are in an unequal relationship, and the sooner you can get out, the better. It can be very difficult to escape from an unequal relationship, particularly if you are having sex with the guy and he is threatening you or if you and he have one or more children and you're concerned about their safety and well-being. The thing is, the longer you are involved in an unequal relationship, the harder it becomes to get out of it.

How Can We Stop It?

To get out of an unequal relationship (or to help your friend do so) you need to enlist the help of an adult, such as a parent. Or, if you can't talk to a parent, talk to another adult, like an aunt or even a teacher you trust.

Once you've lined up an adult ally, you've got to end the relationship. Let the adult know when and where you plan to have this conversation, so he or she can be nearby, or even present, to support you. Tell your partner that you're not happy and you deserve to be treated with respect. He or she may try to get you to stay by promising to change, and the promise might sound very convincing. Don't be sucked in, because you have to remember that it's not necessarily this person's fault that you're in this bad situation. It's just that because of the very nature of your ages and your relationship dynamic, you two are unequal, and no matter how hard he tries to change (assuming he really does try), your relationship will not evolve for the better—it can only get worse.

"I believe that a large age difference in a relationship is a huge issue," says a seventeen-year-old boy. "First, of course, there are the laws that forbid sexual contact between adults and minors. Relationships are complicated enough already without having to wonder if you might be breaking the law every time you go out with your boyfriend or girlfriend. Five years isn't a huge age difference when you're thirty-five and forty, but when you're fifteen and twenty, it's enormous. I myself have changed so completely in the three years from my freshman year of high school to my senior year that I look back and honestly can't even identify with myself. Maybe not everyone changes that much, but the differences in attitude and maturity between the average fifteen-year-old and the average twenty-year-old are astounding. I think most twenty-year-olds realize this. I believe any older person who gets involved in a sexual relationship with a teen is a creep, or is just doing something extremely stupid and damaging to the younger person. Sure, love happens, but if it's really there, it can wait."

Adults usually think of sexual intercourse as something that should be taken very seriously. But the truth is, teenagers are having sex and even losing their virginity the same way that generations past did: in cars, in basements, in fields, in their bedrooms after their parents have gone to sleep.

And the girls who attract older men tend to be more vulnerable, more insecure, and even more in need of tender loving care than the average teenager. So it should come as no surprise that when an older guy comes along and wants these girls to hook up, their sentiment seems to be "Why not?"

Time after time, Moore says, studies and anecdotal evidence find scary answers to the question "Why didn't you use contraception?" What reasons are girls giving? "I didn't think about it," or "It just happened."

According to Dr. Joe McIlhaney of the Sexual Health Center in Austin, Texas, teenagers who are least likely to have sex are "kids who have good connectedness with their parents." That means if your parents are there for you, you're less desperate to get attention; if your parents tell you not to have sex, you're more likely to listen; and, of course, if your parents keep track of you, you're less likely to have the opportunity to have sex. Teens who feel like their parents are neutral about whether they have sex or whose parents don't pay much attention "are feeling lonely—therefore, they're going to go searching for that need to be met."

It seems obvious, but one thing about teens who are sexually active at an early age have in common is that often, their "parents don't really tell them they shouldn't have sex," says McIlhaney. "When connected parents are very clear with their kids about what they expect from them," he continues, "the kids are more likely to avoid risky behavior."

Joe, 17 · Martinsville, NJ

Joe's a public high school junior who's busy both in school and out. He works at the local video store and coaches girls' football. Joe says he's "one of the more popular kids—have been since freshman year." He's also a self-described jock—a quarterback on the football team. He's an earnest kid, and you can tell he's popular for the right reason: because he's nice to everyone. Joe is the kind of guy who takes away the keys of the drunk guy when he's getting ready to drive home. Joe would never even consider dating a freshman. What makes him different from some of his peers? The very things McIlhaney mentions: his connectedness to his parents and a feeling of responsibility to his community.

At my school, it's common for girls to go out with guys who are older, absolutely—up to three years. There's a bunch of sophomore-senior dating. I'm totally against that—I really don't like that, I think it's wrong. If it's two years, she doesn't really know a lot about things, the girls are just not mature enough. I went to a sophomore party, and the way they act, giggling and stuff, it's a major turnoff. I was like, "You gotta be kidding me; I gotta get out of here." They had some beer and were pretending to be drunk, and it was so annoying.

In that kind of a relationship, the guy is going out with her just to be able to fool around with her—he's taking advantage of her. The age of consent is sixteen in New Jersey. We'll joke around about it—if she's fifteen and he's eighteen, we'll be like, "Oh, you better not do anything." The girl'll want to go out with an older guy because he has a car, then there's the whole social status thing: If you're a sophomore dating a senior, your social status goes sky-high. And maybe it's also because she finds the kids in her grade immature. Sure, they like the guy and all, but what she's really doing is exploiting him for herself: He's making her look better.

I can pretty much talk to my parents about anything—my dad I can talk to about drinking and stuff
like that, but as for drugs, sex . . . they're really
against that. My parents are very against sex before
marriage. They're worried about AIDS and pregnancy
and all the stuff that can mess up your life. I'm careful about all that, though, because I have so much I'm
looking forward to, and I know: One mental lapse and
you can be destroyed for life.

I'm applying to the Air Force Academy, Virginia
Military Institute, and The Citadel. I want to be in the
military. I want to be a pilot—like in *Top Gun*. I love
that story—I live for the movie. I own the soundtrack
and everything. I've taken military flight simulators
and stuff. I really want to do it.

More is being done to try to keep teens from having sex with
adults. In response to the high teen pregnancy statistics, a
lot of states are getting tougher about enforcing the statutory
rape laws. California has been particularly aggressive in
large part because since 1995, California's Statutory Rape
Vertical Prosecution Program has been providing grants to
counties to prosecute statutory rape. (According to reports,
a typical scenario in which the guy is arrested involves a
thirteen-year-old mother and her twenty-five-year-old male
partner.) Some counties, such as San Diego, won't prosecute
statutory rape cases unless there is at least a five-year age
gap between partners (or the girl gets pregnant).

Though some district attorneys argue that once a

guy finds out his eighteen-year-old pal's gone to jail for having sex with a minor, he's going to think twice about doing the same, researchers of behavior patterns and sexuality don't agree. The Guttmacher Institute's Patricia Donovan says that it's a complicated web of factors, such as low self-esteem, poverty, and limited opportunities, that drive men to have sexual relationships with teenagers, and statutory rape laws don't address those issues. "The laws really come after the fact," says Dr. Shiener. "If you pass laws, you're not going to stop something from happening, you're just going to punish someone when it does happen."

There's another interesting twist that goes along with the prosecution frenzy: Even a teenager who has consensual sex with a minor can be charged and convicted of felony sexual assault. So if a nineteen-year-old guy has sex with a sixteen-year-old girl and gets convicted, he'll have to register as a sex offender and have his DNA on file—forever.

Kristen Moore says to stop teen-adult relationships society needs to take a multidisciplinary approach, to mix positive and negative rewards for both the girls and the guys. "How can we motivate men to care about the children that they might produce or the adolescents whose lives they may change?" she asks.

LaWanda Ravoira points out that we're feeling the effects of a lack of community. Many teens don't feel that school is a safe place or one where they want to be, and for too many teens home is no better (for some, it's far worse). To put an end to adult-teen sex, teens need to feel connected to school, communities, and family. A teen girl who feels close enough to her parents to talk about what's going on in her life will feel connected. A girl who is involved in community and school activities will feel a part of something bigger than herself. Joining a team will give her an opportunity to support classmates and teammates, as well as to excel and be praised for a job well done. This way, the girl won't seek approval, acceptance, and love from an older guy, because she'll be getting it at school, in her community, and at home.

Teens Who Have Sex with Adults

July 2001 · Arkadelphia, Arkansas

James Smith is put under house arrest for violating a no-contact order with a seventeen-year-old girl. Smith was accused of having sex with the girl more than twenty times over the previous year. The *Arkansas Democrat-Gazette* reported that Smith had called the girl to say he loved her and to ask her not to testify against him.

August 2000 · Rex, Georgia

A forty-one-year-old California teacher picks up a fifteen-year-old girl and takes her to a hotel for a week before being arrested. The FBI reports that the pair met over the Internet.

July 2000 · St. Petersburg, Florida

A forty-one-year-old teacher is arrested for having sex with a sixteen-year-old student with whom he allegedly had an affair. In 1988, he had allegedly lost his teaching certificate for giving another student alcohol and having sex with her.

April 2000 · Jefferson Barracks, Missouri
Otto Jean, forty-six, an air force sergeant, gets two years in prison for having a sexual relationship with a fifteen-year-old girl.

January 2000 · Phoenix, Arizona
A fifteen-year-old girl, missing from Sonoma, California, since the previous October, is found living at a hotel with a thirty-one-year-old man.

September 1999 · St. Louis, Missouri
School employee Betty Bill, forty-one, a mother of three, faces ninety days in jail for having sex with a fourteen-year-old boy at his house.

March 1999 · Valinda, California
A nineteen-year-old man is arrested for having a sexual relationship with a fourteen-year-old girl he met while he was a leader in the county sheriff's Explorers program.

January 1999 · Rensselaer, New York
Edward Farrell, a forty-year-old police officer, gets six months in jail for having sex with a sixteen-year-old girl.

SCARY STATS

The California Alliance for Statutory Rape Enforcement posts the names and photos of those wanted for statutory rape on the Web at www.wetip.com/wetip/sbstat/sbstagr.htm.

November 1998 · Montgomery, Alabama

Officers investigate a parked car. Inside, they find a male professor taking pictures of a half-dressed sixteen-year-old, who tells police that they'd had sex.

October 1998 · Phoenix, Arizona

A married twenty-six-year-old man is arrested for leaving the country with a thirteen-year-old girl.

October 1998 · Thousand Oaks, California

Azu Perry, twenty-three, and Matthew Beck, nineteen, plead guilty to sex with a minor after an incident with a fifteen-year-old girl who knew them.

August 1998 · Mt. Clemens, Michigan

Rebecca Ann Schroeder, a twenty-eight-year-old teacher, is sentenced to a year in jail for having sex with a thireen-year-old male student.

July 1998 · Hastings, Minnesota

Julie Feil, thirty-two, a former high school teacher, is sentenced to nearly seven years in prison for having sex with a fifteen-year-old boy.

July 1998 · Pasadena, California
The thirty-five-year-old wife of a California mayor is arrested for unlawful sex acts with a minor. She allegedly had sex with a sixteen-year-old family friend she hired to baby-sit for the couple's four children.

March 1998 · Palmdale, California
A twenty-nine-year-old woman pleads no contest to child molestation after having sex with a thirteen-year-old boy. Kathy Ann Hoyt allegedly had sex with the boy in his family's trailer home, where she was staying. When his mother found a note she'd written the boy, she went to the police.

A 1996 survey from the University of Winnipeg revealed that 21.8 percent of athletes surveyed said they'd had sexual intercourse with authority figures. Of those athletes, 8.5 percent reported it was forced, and 20 percent said it happened when they were under sixteen.

An estimated 45 percent of those sentenced to prison for nonrape sexual assaults (statutory rape, forcible sodomy, and molestation) said their victims were twelve years old or younger.

U.S. DEPARTMENT OF JUSTICE

"I really don't think girls who abandon their babies are murderers; they are just desperate. I am a very open-minded person, and I can relate to teens in a situation like that. Approximately a month ago, I was scared I would become one of those girls. My period was about a week late, and I was freaking out, because yes, I had had sex in between my last period and that one. That was not fun. I mean, think about it!

That day it finally came was one of my happiest. Now before you pass judgment, saying I should have been prepared for the consequences, we used every contraceptive imaginable, so we were really not expecting any problems. And now that I look back on the whole ordeal, I believe it was the stress of it all that made me late. I once saw a quote that said 'A good scare is often more effective than good advice.' That is sooo true. We have not had sex since then and don't plan to until we are able to support a child if that should occur. So I have learned.

And I can say to other teens reading this: Please wait for sex. I mean, I realized the worst after the fact, and I was lucky nothing happened. My life would be ruined if I had a kid; I am so not ready for that kind of responsibility."

—Sophie, 17

Chapter 5

A Deadly Secret:
Infanticide

In New Jersey, on November 12, 1996, Amy Grossberg, a Bergen County College student, gave birth to a baby boy in a motel room with the help of her boyfriend, Brian Peterson. Brian wrapped the baby in plastic bags, took him outside, and tossed him into a Dumpster. The two teenagers didn't know that they were supposed to deliver the placenta—the sac inside the uterus from which the fetus receives all its nourishment—so a day later Grossberg began hemorrhaging and had to go to the hospital, where doctors determined she'd just given birth. Grossberg and Peterson both accepted plea bargains: Grossberg got two and a half years, Peterson, two years.

Again in New Jersey, on June 6, 1997, high school senior Melissa Drexler gave birth in the bathroom of a catering hall at her prom. She fished her baby out of a toilet bowl, wrapped him in a plastic bag, and, it has been speculated, used the rough edge of a tampon machine to sever the umbilical cord. She then dumped him in the restroom trash. Some newspapers reported that Melissa went back to the dance, requested a song from the DJ, and danced the night away. More recent (and more believable) reports say that Melissa told her friends she wasn't feeling well and went home a little early.

Later that evening, custodians called to clean up the blood in the bathroom discovered the dead infant. Two years after the incident, Melissa read a handwritten statement out loud in court stating she was fully aware that her baby was born alive and that she also knew she would likely cause its death by throwing it in the trash. Melissa was sentenced to fifteen years in prison; according to legal experts she'll probably serve about three.

In February 1996, a tiny baby was found dead on the doorstep of a Poplar Grove, Illinois, residence. Poplar Grove (about seventy miles from Chicago) is a town of seven hundred fifty people, so the question of whose baby this was became quite a town mystery. The town named the ill-fated infant Angelica Faith and even arranged a funeral with a donated tiny tombstone to be placed at the head of her casket. At the funeral was sixteen-year-old Kelli Moye—then a ninth grader—and both of Kelli's parents. Three years later, police got new clues that led them to discover that it had been Kelli's baby.

Kelli had dressed in baggy clothes and concealed her pregnancy from everyone—even her parents. Then she had quietly given birth in her upstairs bedroom while her parents slept downstairs. After that, police say, Kelli bathed the baby, dressed her in pajamas, wrapped her in a towel, and left her on the back steps of the house next door, where the infant died of exposure. Kelli was sentenced to four years in prison after being convicted of manslaughter.

What's Going On Here?

Rahway, New Jersey. Scotts, Michigan. Olathe, Colorado. Across the country, tales emerge of hidden pregnancies, bloody and secret deliveries, and grotesque disposals of the infants. In cases where the mother is found, it's often impossible to believe that the sweet-faced teenage girl could be capable of such a terrible crime. Infanticide is pretty rare in America, but it does happen about two hundred and fifty times a year to children under the age of one. Often the mothers are aged sixteen to twenty-one; the vast majority are teenagers.

Why is this happening? A fifteen-year-old girl sees it this way: "One day, the girl gets pregnant," she says. "She, with her out-of-control mind, will get hectic. Many won't want to tell their parents. Others wouldn't want to lose their boyfriends. And then there are some who could just care less. And so they come to a conclusion . . . trash the baby. I think there should be more advertisements and other things to let these girls know that there are other options. Murder is murder. Perhaps the punishment should be less severe, but the girl would definitely need psychiatric help."

There's a difference in the psychology of girls and women who kill their babies right after giving birth and those who murder them when they're days or weeks old. The psychologist who determined this, Phillip Resnick, coined the term "neonaticide" to mean killing a baby the day it's born, and "filicide" to mean killing a baby who's older than twenty-four hours. Both crimes are referred to as infanticide. This chapter is about neonaticide, since in all the cases discussed, the babies were killed right after they were born.

Though many girls come from supportive families who would be understanding and helpful in case of an accidental pregnancy, others do not. For these girls, who have nowhere to turn (or feel they have nowhere to turn even if that's not really the case), infanticide may seem like the only option.

Roseanne, 18 · Portland, OR

Roseanne is an eighteen-year-old with one child and another on the way. She has gray eyes and an easy smile. She's been living on her own for two years now because her parents kicked her out when they learned she was pregnant.

My daughter is two years old. Giving birth was the most horrible experience in the world. I decided to have it naturally, but next time I am having an epidural. When I saw the baby, I felt like I had just given birth to an angel. I had no one there. The father was too busy getting drunk. He was a drunk and abusive. He gave me a broken nose three times, a hell of a broken arm, and five broken fingers. I'm on Zoloft. I have been depressed my whole life because of an imbalance in my brain. I considered suicide, but then realized, What would it be for? And I would never have the guts to do it. With a lot of people, they have no one to turn to. I had to go to a counselor. I realized my baby needed me, and that is the most important fact of all. Now I'm pregnant again, as the result of sexual abuse.

Yeah, it is hard. It hurts to think that I won't get to go out and do teenage things like sleepovers, teen clubs, boyfriends. When I discovered I was pregnant, I was a sophomore in high school and was head cheerleader. It was hard having everything and then dropping it like a million shattered dreams as sharp as glass. I remember when I used to laugh so hard I couldn't breathe; I'd have to gasp for air. It has been forever since that happened.

Some girls are just not up to it. They are scared to take the consequences. Teenagers should not do what they are tempted to do so much. Sex is like a treat that some teens cannot live without, and that is sad. But women who leave their kids aren't crazy, not at all. They are just teens who are not fully developed mentally. Trying to raise a child when they are not mentally ready is too hard, and they know it.

Dr. Jonas Rappaport, a now-retired psychiatrist who was one of the founders of the American Academy for Forensic Psychiatry, believes that some girls who commit infanticide honestly have no idea they're pregnant, and that their denial is so complete they actually don't even *look* pregnant. In one case, Rappaport says, a girl was on the beach wearing a bikini just a week before her delivery, and no one—not her family, not her friends, no one—suspected she was pregnant.

And just in case you were thinking that these girls are heartless young women who are having sex left and right, that's not true. "These are not loose girls," Rappaport says. "These are girls from nice families who had mothers who said, 'You can always come to me if you're in trouble.'" Rappaport goes on to say that the majority of girls in the eight infanticide cases he studied had a supportive mother as well as aunts and teachers who they could have confided in. That's one of the arguments, he says, for the theory that the girls themselves are completely unaware of the pregnancy— they could have confided in an adult, but they didn't because they didn't know they had reason to.

Often these girls won't have any memory of the birth or of killing the child, says Rappaport. They only remember being arrested and taken away. It seems hard to believe that a young woman could be pregnant for nine months and then be shocked when the birth occurs, but apparently it happens. In fact, that would explain why Melissa Drexler could give birth at the prom and then return to her friends and act pretty normally, if a little under the weather. But what about the Amy Grossberg/Brian Peterson killing? "That was different," Rappaport says. "Since he was in on it, it couldn't have been an unconscious neonaticide."

"Those girls just got scared," says a seventeen-year-old girl. "Some of them are probably mental, but most just don't know where to turn. When they were carrying the child, it was like a dream, something they could just ignore until later. It was a rose-colored view of motherhood. When the mother has the child, however, it's a kick in the ass. They get a good dose of reality. I can empathize some, but there are better ways of dealing than abandonment. Do you know how many people would kill for a child?"

According to Rappaport, teens who commit infanticide actually block out the situation, much like a person in a car crash who can't remember anything about that day, or a victim of sexual abuse who doesn't recall it. But if you don't believe the unconscious-neonaticide theory, you're not alone: Most of the girls Rappaport testified for ended up with prison terms. "It's a very hard thing to convince people of," he says. "But I believe it to be true."

Who's Doing This?

Though there have been more reports lately of infanticides in upper-middle-class communities, a 1998 study by Dr. Mary Overpeck showed that babies of poor, unwed teenagers who already have one or more children are at greatest risk of infanticide. This may be because these are the young women who have the least social support and feel the most desperate about their circumstances.

What are these girls thinking? A better question might be: Are they even thinking at all? According to Neil Kaye, a forensic psychologist who has studied infanticide extensively, "The girl can't admit the pregnancy to herself or her family because she's ashamed and she fears punishment or rejection. So basically, she goes into denial." You've probably heard the word "denial" before, as in "You think you're going to get into Yale? You're in denial about your grades." Or "Can't you see that your boyfriend has a drug problem? You must be in denial." While it's true that people who don't seem to notice or care about their situation may just not want to admit the truth, even to themselves, these girls suffer from a more intense kind of denial. They really, truly, in their hearts, convince themselves that they're not pregnant.

"These girls honestly feel," Kaye says, "that 'If I deny it, it'll go away.' Usually even the father does not know the girl is pregnant." Denial this complete, according to Kaye, usually stems from fear.

What are they afraid of? Lots of things—some real, others imagined. They're afraid of being kicked out of their homes and rejected by their parents, their families, their friends, their communities. They're afraid of childbirth and parenthood, they're afraid of having an abortion, and they're almost more afraid of people finding out about an abortion if they were to have one. In this panic they think, "This can't be happening to me. There must be a mistake. I am not pregnant." In fact, teenagers tend to have strong stomach muscles, which means they are less likely to show a pregnancy until it is far along, unlike women in their twenties or thirties, who usually begin to look pregnant after three to four months.

"Girls who do things like that aren't thinking. There's a lot of emotional trauma with getting pregnant and actually having the baby; the girls are very, very disoriented," says a sixteen-year-old girl. "They could probably all claim temporary insanity because of the stress level. I don't think it's murderous unless it's premeditated, if the girl knows that she's going to ditch the baby in a trash can before she actually has it."

Dr. Kaye says that some mothers are suffering from psychosis when they kill their children. You've probably heard of postpartum depression, which is a state of mind that some mothers go through after childbirth—it's attributed to both her changing hormones and the way her entire life has changed since she became responsible for a child. A mother in the throes of postpartum depression might feel weepy, down in the dumps, even hopeless for weeks on end. A more extreme (and extremely rare) form of postpartum depression is postpartum psychosis, which actually could cause a woman to harm her child.

Besides feelings of denial, what else do these girls have in common? They are usually not psychotic or depressed. They almost never attempt suicide. They almost never seek prenatal care. When you ask them whose idea it was to have sex in the first place, they generally feel it was forced on them rather than something they initiated. They almost never go on to kill other children or harm anyone else. In fact, studies show that these girls can become loving mothers in the future.

Why Now?

As far back as 1643, Massachusetts law stated that the punishment for killing a "bastard child" was death—proof that infanticide is no new issue. Historically, migratory societies have killed babies born in multiples so the mother could preserve enough resources to adequately care for her other children. Hunter-gatherer societies, anthropologists have determined, also killed newborns who were sick or disabled or born too soon after a brother or sister for the same reason—so the mother could conserve her resources to care for the healthy children she already had.

The number of teen moms killing their babies is not increasing, though the demographics may be shifting to include more girls from upper-middle-class families, which always sparks more media attention than the same circumstances in poor communities. But while the number of infanticides per year has remained relatively constant, the media coverage of this tragedy has increased, so awareness is greater. Still, experts believe there are many cases no one ever finds out about. Often a pregnant girl will confide only in her best friend, who feels obligated to keep the news a secret. The friend likely doesn't realize that the pregnant girl and the baby may be at great risk since neither is likely to receive prenatal care or even birthing assistance.

Janice, 14 · Columbus, OH

Janice is a high school girl who's waiting to have sex. She used to fight with her parents a lot, but these days they're getting along. Janice attributes the change to everyone focusing on better communication. She was raised to be religious and feels her relationship with God helps her make important decisions.

I don't believe it was right for those girls to kill the babies. They made the decision to have sex, so they should know the consequences of having sex. Especially if they chose not to protect themselves, they knew the outcome of what they were doing. It's a really selfish act to kill the child. They had other options; they could have given it up for adoption, because there are many people out there who can't have kids. I think they should be punished for it: life in prison.

There are a few pregnant people at our school; there are a few that already have children. But it's not a really high number, maybe ten. We're freshmen this year, and in seventh grade, there was this one girl— she was my cousin's best friend—they were in sixth grade and she got pregnant but nobody knew. She had her baby at the very beginning of her seventh-grade year. It like freaked everybody out because she was so young. We really didn't think it was possible. I mean, we knew, but you know, we didn't know. She hid it by wearing baggy clothes, things like that. She wasn't showing very much.

She still has the baby. Her mother and father are helping her take care of the baby. They're very supportive of her, but they're like mad she didn't tell them. They were supportive once she made the decision to tell them and that she wanted to keep the baby. The baby's father isn't around.

When that happened, it hit me in the head, like "Oh wow, this is really real. Someone that I know so well is actually—you know." It's kind of scary. You hear stories in the news about how girls hide their pregnancies or you read about it in the magazines, but when someone close to you does it, it's kind of scary. We asked her, like, did you know that you were pregnant? But she didn't say anything. She really didn't want to comment on it.

I think she was depressed, 'cause no one really saw her in the summertime, and in the beginning of the year when school started she didn't come to school. We didn't know what was going on. I really think she was ashamed and embarrassed.

Her parents, they're not really strict. Maybe if they were a bit stricter she wouldn't have been in that situation. But they're really easy to talk to, and she gets along with them now. Like I said, they're really supportive of her, but I think if she had told her parents earlier in the pregnancy, I'm not sure if they would have let her keep the baby.

If I got pregnant? I have no idea, I really don't. I mean, I would be really disappointed in myself. And I'm sure a lot of other people would be disappointed in me as well. I don't think I could give my baby up for adoption. I mean, nine months of carrying a child that's yours, that you created, and, you know, giving birth and then giving it to someone else? That's a hard thing to do, so I don't think that would be an option for me. In most circumstances, I don't agree with abortion. I believe that if you're old enough to have sex, or if you think you're mature enough, you should be mature enough to face the consequences.

I am choosing to wait to have sex. I have a few friends that are virgins, but I have a few more that aren't. It's more common that they aren't than that they are, at fourteen, fifteen. They say sex is really not all that it's cracked up to be. Some of them are careful, they're on the Pill, or their parents put them on the Pill or there's places where you can get condoms really easy around our school; you can go talk to a counselor, you know, they have them there. A lot of kids don't want to come out and tell people that they're having sex, but they want to be able to protect themselves, so when protection is made available, I think it's easier for them. I don't think they feel as ashamed as if they had to buy condoms in the store.

My mother and father are really supportive of the things that I do, and we have a really strong trust in our relationship. I don't lie to my parents, I tell them everything, you know, if they ask. Some things I don't volunteer; as a teenager your parents aren't your best friends, so you don't tell them all your secrets, but if they ask me then I tell them the truth. I think if parents are more open-minded and listen to what their kids are saying rather than telling them what it's going to be like, the kids would be more apt to tell the parents the things they're doing or how they feel about certain issues. When you cut a child off, tell them what you think before they're finished, you just shut them off and they don't want to talk to you anymore.

Well, I think if you are pregnant, you have to be able to talk to your parents. If you can't go to a parent, you should be able to go to someone. Teens have to trust someone. I know it's really hard, and they feel no one understands them. I used to think like that too. But my parents were my age at one point. The things that are going on now may be a little more explicit than they were then, but I'm sure they have some similarities. Your parents can help you, and they do have some pretty good advice. You might think they don't understand and they'll never understand, or you may think what they're telling you is bogus and not going to help at all, but if you wait a while and listen, what they say is often true.

Teens that are pregnant obviously weren't afraid to have sex, so they should take the responsibility to get prenatal care and stuff like that. Kids don't ask to be brought into the world; the least you could do is take care of your child.

What Are the Signs?

When teenage mothers commit infanticide, says Dr. Kaye, it's because the pregnancy was unwanted, it occurred out of wedlock, and the girl feels ashamed—enough so that she keeps the pregnancy a secret. This girl has, through her parents or her friends or her teachers or even just her own experience, somehow gotten the message that teen pregnancy is so shameful, so not-done, that she'll be tossed out of her home if anyone finds out.

The girl may continue to live her life as normally as possible, dressing in baggy clothes to hide her swelling stomach and possibly even mistaking spotting (which is common during pregnancy) for her period. Or it's equally possible that a teenage girl has such an irregular period that it doesn't seem so abnormal for her to stop getting it for months on end. To this girl, the fetus is not a potential baby, it's a "thing" inside her. A thing that, says Dr. Kaye, she has no more affection for than she has for last night's dinner passing through her intestines.

But then comes the birth. Until that moment, "some of these girls really don't know they're pregnant," says Dr.

Kaye. "Either they're so unsophisticated or their denial has been so complete" that they're astonished when they give birth. At this point, the girl experiences a kind of dementia because she's been telling herself she's not pregnant, yet clearly she can see that she's giving birth to a baby. This kind of reality clash, when you believe something to be true even though all the signs around you point to the opposite conclusion, is called cognitive dissonance. As you can imagine, it's a very, very scary feeling to have.

"Very few pregnant teenagers can really handle what is happening to them without someone to guide them and make them aware of the options available," says a nineteen-year-old girl. "Heck, most pregnant *women* need that sort of assistance as well, but they find it in their doctors and family members. These girls are so frightened, they don't get the kind of support all pregnant women need."

This ashamed, terrified, confused girl has just given birth. "If anyone finds out," she reasons, "I'll be thrown out of my house, shunned by my friends and my community." So she does to the baby what she fears will be done to her: She gets rid of it. The number one method teen girls use when committing infanticide, according to Dr. Kaye, is drowning. Why? Because it's common that these secret pregnancies are delivered into a toilet, so if the girl is just passive after the birth, she can let the water drown the baby. The second most common infanticide method is exposure: leaving the baby on a doorstep or leaving it near trash or even in a Dumpster, as Amy Grossberg and Brian Peterson did. In this way the girls rid themselves of the baby without really doing anything aggressive to make it die. Some girls might even honestly believe that the babies will be found and cared for.

"I feel that a lot of people who abandon their baby have no other options, or perhaps are unable to think of any," says a fifteen-year-old girl. "Having to go to school, or having a job, and having a baby would be tough. I know in my school, many girls actually carry babies with them, because they have nowhere else to leave them. I must give them credit, though, because they didn't quit school and are trying to keep their lives going. There are options, and one should decide in the beginning whether they can take care of a baby and handle all the responsibility. There should always be an alternative to leaving a baby in an alley, whether it be foster care or even an abortion. Teens should make good decisions from the start, rather than having to do possibly the worst possible thing in the end."

Antonia, 16 · South Bend, IN

Antonia comes from a big Italian family with a sister, three brothers, and nine nieces and nephews. After dropping out for a while, she just started going back to school. Antonia and her boyfriend, Bill, were expecting their first child soon.

This is not the first time I have been pregnant; however, this is the first one that will be born. When I was fourteen, I got pregnant with my first love's baby. He was eighteen. The baby was located in my tubes, so I couldn't carry it. When I found out I was pregnant this time, I didn't really know what to think. My boyfriend and I had been arguing like crazy, and it was rough. I was under a lot of stress, and I thought my period wasn't coming because of the stress. I really didn't think I was pregnant. It never crossed my mind until one of my best friends, Amy, came over and said she had a dream that I was pregnant. So we went and bought one of those home test things and did it at my house, with my boyfriend here. When it was time to read the test, and it said positive, I about died. My first reaction was to cry, but I didn't. I showed the stick to Amy and Bill. Amy cried; Bill didn't know what to think. From that day, everywhere we went, Bill held my arms so I wouldn't fall.

Amy was very supportive, but just to make sure the test was for real, I went to a women's care center to take one of their tests. When it returned with the same answer, I thought for sure it was all wrong. I do sympathize with these girls who kill their children. Society has made it so hard to be a teen mom that it is unbelievable. Adults look down at you like you are trash, but you're not. You made a mistake, just like they have at some point in their lives. It is hard enough raising a baby without someone breathing down your neck about what your mistake was. You already have the baby. You have to take care of it every day. Why should you have to have people looking in your eyes with disgust? Others should mind their own business and accept the fact that this has happened.

My father and my grandfather are really big on education, and they both think relationships should come last in your adolescent life. When my father found out I was pregnant, he was not too happy at all. Unfortunately, I have no relationship with my grandpa, I believe because I'm pregnant. My oldest brother, John, has no children but is married. My brother Jeff has four kids; my sister has five. My mom is very supportive. I have no doubt that if I ever need them for anything, my family will always be there.

When that first doctor's appointment came where Bill, my mother, and I got to hear the baby's heartbeat, I knew that was what I wanted. I know it will be hard, but I have a lot of people who will be there for me, so I know that even at my lowest point, I will always have someone to help pick me back up.

Right now my life has a ton of ups and downs. My parents will be going through a divorce soon, and the pressure between them about who me and my younger brother will live with sometimes gets bad. Things between my boyfriend and me are rough too, but we will get through it. I love him very much. I have a lot of stress around me all the time, so it's kind of hard to vent because the emotions are so high here.

I currently am back in school. It took a long while for me to realize where I needed to be. With some pushes from my parents, my boyfriend, and my best friends, I am back on track and am reaching for my goal of becoming some sort of counselor. I was depressed for a while. It took me running away, skipping school, drinking, and being around the wrong people for me to come home and see how badly I'd hurt my friends and my mom. My friends were even going around to strangers' houses and knocking on doors trying to find me. I could have lost every single one of them, but I have real friends, and they were the ones who stuck by me.

Some people think, "You're too young to do it," but there is no age that is too young. Just because you weren't careful doesn't mean you don't have the inner strength to carry on throughout it.

How Can We Stop It?

If you have a teen friend and you suspect she might be pregnant, ask her about it. You don't have to be accusing (that will only make her defensive); just bring up the topic casually, maybe by asking her what she would do if she ever accidentally became pregnant. If she won't answer the question or she freaks out, you should talk with her more directly about what's going on and get an adult involved—in a case like this your instincts are probably right. Encourage her to talk to an adult she trusts, and you should do the same—you don't want to be the only one who knows about it. It's too much of a burden for you to try to be responsible for your friend's health or that of her baby. If you're not sure who to talk to, call a local Planned Parenthood. They can discuss care and options with your friend confidentially, and they charge on a sliding-scale fee (which means she pays only what she can afford).

But if someone you know does conceal a pregnancy and you don't catch on until it's too late, know that it's not your fault. Even infanticide experts say it can be extremely difficult or even impossible to recognize a girl who is concealing a pregnancy because she is in denial about it. She will be very convincing when she lists all the reasons why she could not possibly be pregnant.

Obviously, in cases of infanticide when the mothers don't even know they're pregnant, there's no way to prevent it. But for the majority of the girls, the ones who feel too ashamed or humiliated to talk to their parents or another adult, there are steps we can take. Perhaps unintentionally, some parents are sending a dangerous message: If you act in a way that disappoints me, I won't love you anymore. "The message," says Dr. Kaye, "is that every parent should say, 'Look, I don't care what you do—if you really screw up I'm going to be mad, but I'll still be your parent and I'll help you out and I'll still love you.' " It's not enough to be vague, though. Parents should even give examples of how they would come to the rescue in any situation, even the ones listed in this book. As much as no parents want to believe their kid will ever be in this situation, some parents will have to face it. In that case, it's better for the parents to hear about the situation from their kid directly.

Many times girls (and guys) talk about pregnancy (or other big issues) and they say, "If my parents knew, they'd kill me." Most of the time, with prodding, girls will admit that okay, their parents probably won't really kill them, but they will be massively disappointed, which almost seems worse. Then there is a small population of girls whose parents are walking time bombs and could actually explode violently over news like this.

If your parents have never talked to you about how to deal if you find yourself in a crisis, bring it up! You don't have to freak them out—just ask them what they would want you to do if, say, a friend was pregnant. It's likely your parents will give you the "Please come to me first if ever you need help" speech. If they say it—believe them! They mean it. But if they don't, you should seek out an adult you trust (an older sister? a cool aunt?) to ask her if you could call her if you were ever really, really in major trouble. The thing is, you always have options. It's just a matter of knowing what those options are. An important first step toward finding out what your choices are is talking to someone older and wiser before you make any major life-altering decisions. If you ever feel you have no one to turn to, try calling a teen hot line such as 1-800-4-A-CHILD, where trained volunteers can help you figure out what to do.

"My brother's girlfriend has a four-year-old, and she's twenty," says an eighteen-year-old boy. "It's hard, but it's possible. They're doing well, and she even got her diploma. They have a house and a brand-new car. If the parents are dedicated, it can be done. But girls who abandon their kids—that's completely messed up. When a father leaves his kid, he's a bad guy, but people don't really care anymore. But if he's a single father raising a child, it's a miracle. Parents shouldn't be rewarded for raising their kids like they're supposed to. If a parent—either parent—leaves a child, they're definitely mentally ill."

This brings up a good point, which is that girls who find themselves pregnant are expected to deal with this problem themselves. It's far more unusual to see guys being held accountable (by girls, by parents, by communities) for pregnancies, even though they are, after all, equally responsible. It's important that parents stress to their son that if he gets a girl pregnant, he will suffer consequences—there's no get-out-of-jail-free card just because he won't be the one to actually give birth.

"I have had coworkers in their teens who were either pregnant or had girlfriends they got pregnant," says a seventeen-year-old boy. "One is still pregnant; the other has a one-year-old baby boy. The problem with teen pregnancy is that often it happens in a relationship where the boy and girl aren't committed to each other. The boy may break up with the girl, and that might cause her, in her distress, to dump the baby. I can't blame the mother. She obviously can't be thinking properly to do such a thing."

Another thing experts agree on is that doctors who treat adolescent girls need to ask them tactful yet detailed questions to figure out whether a girl is pregnant. Some girls who commit neonaticide have seen a doctor for some other reason during their pregnancy, but the doctor didn't ask about the possibility of pregnancy, so the girls didn't bring it up either.

Thomas, 19 • Greensboro, PA
Thomas is a high school senior who hates school. He'd rather be learning programming languages or messing around on the computer, which is what he does in his spare time. He lives with his grandmother and takes care of her. He's thinking of going to technical school or college next year.

I think people want a way out. A lot of people are way too pressured. Not just by schools, but by parents and their peers also. Way too much is expected of teens, socially and academically. I hate the pressure of being expected to make great grades and hate the pressure of my peers expecting me to be social along with it.

I'm going to be seeing a mental health professional about my severe depression and low self-esteem. I've been in a depression for over two years and actually wanted to commit suicide a few times. But I see I need help now—especially with the new addition coming soon. I want a healthy environment for my child.

When I found out I was going to be a teen dad, I was pretty shocked and in disbelief. My fiancée and I are not really ready for another addition to our relationship. Although we aren't ready, we are taking responsibility and are going to raise the child and show him or her a lot of love. We don't want the child to feel like a mistake.

I think a lot of girls try to hide their pregnancies because they are scared. It just shows that society is way too hard on teens over a natural thing. Reproduction is all instinct, while society takes it further than that. Society condemns those who don't conform to the standards, and in all honesty, these girls have a right to be scared. Society changes, while the reproductive cycle doesn't. Although I am understanding, that doesn't mean I condone it. I think not only for their health, but their child's health, they should make sure people know, so they can be helped.

Teen moms who abandon their children fear they have no one to go to and sometimes feel it would be better for the child. In my opinion, only a few actually "forget" their motherly instincts out of selfishness and abandon their child. No matter what, though, there is always help. There's no need to abandon a baby. It may take a while, but don't give up hope. I think if a teen abandons their child, they have to be mentally ill. That goes for anyone who abandons a child. If our instincts fail us, there is something wrong mentally somewhere.

In April 1999, a shy, studious thirteen-year-old eighth-grade girl in Elizabethtown, Pennsylvania, secretly gave birth to a baby girl in her family's bathroom. She wrapped the baby in a plastic bag and hid her in a cold basement cabinet. It's not clear whether she suffocated the baby with her hands or the baby suffocated inside the plastic bag, but two days later, she started having physical problems, so her parents took her to Hershey Medical Center. There, a doctor figured out that she'd just given birth and notified local police, who then searched her house and found the baby's hidden body.

Under Pennsylvania law, all teenagers charged with homicide are automatically treated as adults; it is up to the defense attorney to convince authorities to pursue juvenile charges. In this case, however, prosecutors decided not to charge the girl as an adult. (Had she been, she would have become the youngest girl ever charged as an adult in Lancaster County.)

As punishment for girls who commit infanticide,

Kaye says, "incarceration is a waste of time and money. Incarceration is to protect the public, but there's no likelihood these girls will reoffend." Some experts think imprisoning girls for infanticide will act as a deterrent for other girls who are considering the crime. That argument, Kaye says, is faulty. "No girl would do this if she thought she had other options." In Britain, girls and women who commit infanticide are viewed as mentally ill and get treatment, not prison sentences.

"Some girls, I understand, are so stressed out that they go temporarily insane. They don't know what they're doing, they can't handle it," says a seventeen-year-old boy. "Those girls will probably regret it for the rest of their lives once they realize what they've done. You really don't have to punish those girls, since they'll punish themselves forever. Those are the girls who will need some serious counseling. There are other girls, however, who just flat-out don't care. They didn't have the foresight to prevent it: They didn't get an abortion because that would cost money; they didn't take the Pill; they didn't care enough to put the kid up for adoption. Those are the ones who, in my opinion, ought to be punished. If they don't care for their own child, how can you be sure that they won't kill someone else inconvenient to their lives?"

In America, two thirds of women and girls who commit infanticide in our six largest cities aren't given prison terms, according to a study by criminologist Coromae Richey Mann. Those who are convicted receive an average sentence of seven years.

"I just fully don't respect anyone who would kill a

SCARY STATS

child," says a fourteen-year-old girl. "I know they do that out of desperation, but how could you live with yourself? I would just be thinking about it all the time, and it would most likely drive me insane. I think they should get help before they do that. Here where I live there is a home for that kind of thing. A mother can leave a baby there and she doesn't have to leave a name or anything. They'll take care of it for three months, and when the three months are up they'll put the child up for adoption. I think it is a great thing, and it really has lowered the number of teens abandoning their babies."

Twenty-eight states are considering "safe abandonment" legislation that would allow mothers to give up their children anonymously without fear of punishment. The movement took off after activists responded to the plight of a Mobile, Alabama, boy delivered and left in a toilet.

There are also individual counties, including Lancaster, Pennsylvania, the town where Nicole Boyer hid her baby in the basement, that are placing baskets in or near hospitals where mothers can anonymously deposit babies and take off, no questions asked. In Dakota County, Minnesota, the Safe Place Program has hospitals where mothers can deposit unharmed newborns and walk away. In Texas, the Harris County Baby Abandonment Task Force erected highway billboards that say "Don't abandon your baby. Save your baby."

Teens Abandoning Babies

July 2001 · Beverly Hills, California

A nineteen-year-old girl is sentenced to six years in prison for the death of her newborn son, who was found in a trash bin.

April 2001 · Margate, Florida

An eleven-year-old boy is fishing near his grandmother's house when his line hooks onto a package. Inside is a dead baby.

August 2000 · Omaha, Nebraska

A fourteen-year-old girl is charged with manslaughter. She and her mother had brought her sixteen-

Twenty-nine states require a teenager seeking an abortion to notify or get permission from one of her parents.

ALAN GUTTMACHER INSTITUTE

A survey of girls who'd had abortions found that 61 percent had told their parents beforehand.

PLANNED PARENTHOOD

As many as 10 percent of mothers experience postpartum depression; up to 85 percent experience some form of blues after giving birth; medicine, alone or with therapy, can alleviate symptoms.

AMERICAN FAMILY PHYSICIAN

Twenty percent of sexually active teen girls get pregnant each year; 78 percent of these pregnancies are unintentional.

ALAN GUTTMACHER INSTITUTE

Between 30 and 40 percent of teenage pregnancies are aborted. The rate is highest in New Jersey, where over half of teen pregnancies end in abortion, and lowest in Utah, where it's about 15 percent.

ALAN GUTTMACHER INSTITUTE

Forty-five percent of homicides of children under one year old are committed within the first twenty-four hours after birth.

AMERICAN ACADEMY OF FAMILY PHYSICIANS

Of juvenile murder victims aged five and under, 54 percent were killed by a parent.

U.S. DEPARTMENT OF JUSTICE

hour-old dead newborn to the hospital. An autopsy revealed that the infant had been born alive.

April 2000 · Quincy, Florida
A dog pulls out the charred remains of a baby from a trash fire. The infant is traced to a fifteen-year-old girl in the neighborhood who concealed her pregnancy. She says the child was stillborn, so she wrapped it in a sheet and threw it in a pile of trash. A twenty-one-year-old man is arrested for her rape.

August 1999 · New York
A nineteen-year-old girl gets one to three years for causing the death of her newborn son. She had been a University of Buffalo student, a violinist, and a gymnast. Her parents were not aware of her pregnancy.

February 1999 · Minneola, Florida
A newborn boy is left outside a church. An attached note says that the mother is a seventeen-year-old who can't feed him. "Please help," it reads.

"I've had a pretty good life. My parents both love me very much; I have four older brothers who are very protective and would do anything for me. But, well, my mother is an alcoholic. As I type this, she is upstairs, passed out. I know there is nothing I can do. She has to get out of this herself.

But I have another problem. You've probably heard in the news about cutters—people who cut themselves when they're depressed because it makes them feel better? Well, I do that. I've been trying to get myself out of it, but I just get these urges. I have scars all over my legs and arms, and recently I started cutting my leg again. I went to the school guidance counselor and talked to her, and she called my parents.

Wanna know what they did? Nothing. They didn't want to believe that there was a problem with their youngest child and only daughter. So I'm stuck. I don't know what to do. I don't know what I can do. I told my best friend, and she threatened to beat me up if I did it again. But I did it anyway, and she gave me a black eye. I admire it in the mirror. Why do I like pain? I don't know. Maybe I'm crazy. I don't know what's wrong with me."

—Julie, 16

Chapter 6

Alone and in Pain:
Self-Injury

Sᴀsʜᴀ ʀᴇᴍᴇᴍʙᴇʀs ᴛʜᴇ ғɪʀsᴛ ᴛɪᴍᴇ she cut. She was thirteen years old, and school wasn't going well. She'd been held back in grade school, and since then, she didn't really have too many friends. OCD, ADD: all these letters meant to her was that she didn't fit in. When middle school came, things got really bad. People would trip her in the hall, refuse to talk to her, call her a lesbian.

Her parents knew things weren't great, but she didn't want to bring them down by telling them exactly how unpopular she was. And besides, she'd never been that close to her mom, and her dad drank a lot. Though she was only in the fifth grade, she started having fantasies about ending it all. She told herself she could never do it, but it was interesting to think about. One day after school, when she was home alone in the kitchen, she picked up a knife. She knew she didn't want to die, but she wanted to see what she could do. Holding the knife with her right hand, she made a cut on her left shoulder, just enough to make it bleed—just enough to watch it bleed.

Weirdly, and to her own surprise, instead of feeling pain,

Sasha felt better. For years, she'd been keeping things inside. When she cut, suddenly it was like all of those feelings were leaving her body through the wound she'd made. Finally, she had a way to express her hurt. Cutting stayed Sasha's secret through high school and into college. When the kids at school made fun of her, she cut. When she started to remember an incident of abuse from her father, she cut. When college was harder than high school, she cut. When she had trouble making friends, she cut. When she started feeling attracted to a girl, she cut.

Sasha's story of self-injury ended in her third year at a Christian college. She'd been stressing about a relationship, so she cut her wrist. Her friends made her go to the hospital. There was no hope of playing it off, since just a few days earlier she'd been sent to the ER with a cut on her other wrist. They'd glued the cut closed and sent her on her way. This time, she wasn't getting off so easily. The hospital made her go to the psych ward. The staff told her school. Her school made her leave. Her new school wouldn't take her old credits. She's twenty-three and a freshman. Sasha lost everything and has to start over—all because she cut. All because she didn't know how to say "I'm angry" or "Help me."

What's Going On Here?

It's more common than you'd think—teenagers purposely cutting, burning, scratching, or hitting themselves. Most people's first reaction is that it's a suicide attempt. In fact, say doctors, that's usually not the case. Self-injurers, often called cutters, use physical pain to help them deal with emotional pain.

"It's a coping mechanism," says Tracy Alderman, Ph.D., a San Diego psychologist and author of *The Scarred Soul: Understanding and Ending Self-Inflicted Violence.* A girl gets upset. She's never learned how to speak up, so she needs to find another release for her feelings. The feelings can come from a variety of places. Many (but not all) cutters were victims of child sexual abuse that they never talked about. When a frustrated, unhappy girl cuts herself, she feels a wash of emotion, the same way she might feel if she'd yelled at the person who hurt her in the first place.

Or take a boy who has always gotten all As, but one day he fails a test. He feels worthless, and he's scared that he might ruin his chances at a good future. Because he gets so frustrated and he doesn't know what to do with his anger and disappointment, he punches a wall. Suddenly, the pain in his hand replaces the pain he'd been having inside. Bandaging his hand is much easier than working through the mental pain.

"Before I started cutting myself, I'd burn myself," says one sixteen-year-old girl. "I'd get needles really hot and burn myself when I was upset or mad. It'd make me feel better. It was a way of distracting myself, of preoccupying myself until I could calm down and deal with the situation. I had a friend who did it too, and some of my other friends were like, 'You're so cool!' The last couple of times I did it I needed stitches, but I didn't get them, and the cuts just bled for like four days."

Self-abuse has been happening for centuries. In earlier times, people punished themselves for what they considered sinful behavior by whipping themselves or wearing hair shirts. They had religious or moral reasons, but today cutters do it to relieve personal tension—pain that they've never learned how to talk about. In the past few years, several books have been published on the subject, and the USA Network aired a movie called *Secret Cutting*. As more people become aware of this dangerous pattern, more and more teens are coming forward to say that they too have been hurting themselves. In some areas, cutting has even become a macabre trend, on a par with tattoos and piercings. Which brings up another reason why teens cut themselves—some (misguided) people think it's cool that a person can withstand that kind of pain and suffering. When a girl who cuts gets told she's cool for doing it (especially if she's not used to being called cool), she'll keep it up.

"Last year at my school, it was somehow cool to carve your boyfriend's initials into your ankle or your arm," says a twelve-year-old girl. "One friend was saying that she would do it if I did it. I never thought it would be so hard to get out of the pressure. I started to do it, but when I saw my friend's face, I had to stop her as well as stop myself. I was disgusted because I didn't think my friends had any reason to do it except it was the new trend, which to me was awful. But for those people who do it for psychological reasons, it makes sense, because they don't know any other way to escape except to hurt themselves even more."

People self-injure for a number of reasons, the most common of which are: They want to escape feelings of sadness, emptiness, or numbness; they want to ease tension; they are repeating a form of abuse they've suffered; they're enraged; they want to show someone how much they've been hurt; they're afraid of intimacy or responsibility; or they're trying to take control of their body. Some research also indicates that when self-injurers cut themselves, chemicals in the brain get released and act as relaxants, which makes the self-injurer feel better.

Maybe a girl's been shot down by her crush and thinks she's worthless. Burning herself is a way of punishing herself, of expressing how much she hates herself. Maybe she's under tons of pressure to do well because she just got a new student council position. Or she's worried she won't be able to do it all, but she's afraid to tell anyone, so she cuts herself. It makes her feel like she can control something.

In most cases, young people cut their arms or legs, but there are also incidences of self-injurers (SIs) picking at scabs so they don't heal; pulling their hair; putting dangerous objects in their bodies; infecting themselves on purpose; even breaking their own bones.

Jamie, 16 · St. Paul, MN

Jamie is a junior in high school and seems to have the perfect life: She's pretty, and she lives with both of her happily married parents. She also has one sister and one brother—plus a dog, a cat, a rabbit, and an iguana. Jamie enjoys school and is an accomplished flute player. She hopes to attend community college before going on to a university to become an archaeologist, a paleontologist, or an anthropologist. She loves to eat but just lost a lot of weight and is excited about her new look.

Growing up, my younger sister pretty much ran the house. My mom would get mad at her, and then my sister would get mad at the rest of us. One of her freak-outs could cause the house to be silent for days. Now she has medication, so she's not as crazy.

The first time I self-injured was when my history teacher called my parents and told them something I'd said that she considered rude. Since she's an adult and I'm just a kid, my parents sided with her. I'd been depressed for a long time. I was in my room and I just saw this broken glass candleholder, and I cut my arm a few times. I liked it. I started cutting just when I was really depressed. After a while, I cut every day. The bad cuts were all on my arms. The razors I used were really sharp. Once I cut the back of my wrist a bunch of times and I had to go to the emergency room and get butterfly stitches. I have lots of scars from the deep ones.

I used to think about suicide all the time. Self-injuring made me feel better. While I was SI-ing, I was crying, or sometimes I felt happy because I was doing such a good job. A good job means that I was cutting really deep. I know that's sick. Afterward, I felt good. I didn't regret it like most people do.

My teachers told my counselor that I had these cuts, and the counselor tried to help me. I was pissed off because she's a total moron, and I just wanted her to shut up. Last February, though, my parents finally found out that I cut. They were really sad and didn't understand at all. That's when I started going to day treatment at the hospital.

I haven't done it now for about two weeks. That's a long time for me. I don't think I will ever totally stop. If things get bad again, I will definitely cut. People think that cutters want attention. In some cases, it has to do with needing attention, but in most cases people do it because they hate themselves.

I don't know what gave me the idea to do it. When I hear about SI or teen suicide in the media, it pisses me off. They don't know crap about it. They call cutting "the new anorexia." What the hell is that supposed to mean? I found out after I started cutting that a lot of my friends cut too. They weren't as bad as me, though. Most of them had already stopped. It's not like I got the idea from them.

It's hard to understand why someone would intentionally hurt himself or herself. Because it's so confusing, people sometimes come to the wrong conclusions as they try to make sense of cutting. Here are some of the top myths about self-injurers:

- *It's a suicide attempt.* It's true that some self-injurers hurt themselves so badly that they wind up hospitalized or dead. But generally speaking, these people are trying to end just their pain, not their lives. It doesn't sound like it makes sense, but cutters don't want to hurt themselves—they just want to stop hurting. "There's tons of misunderstanding about self-injurers, even in the medical community," says Alderman. "A teen will show up with a cut or burn, and it's automatically seen as suicidal."

- **They can just quit.** Cutting and self-injuring are coping mechanisms for teens who don't know what else to do. Afterward, many cutters experience feelings of guilt or embarrassment, which causes them to hate themselves, which can cause them to want to cut again. This cycle is difficult to break unless the person learns a new way to deal with his or her sadness, anger, or loneliness.

- **It's only for attention.** A lot of people figure that since most of the wounds aren't that deep, the cutters must be looking for attention. But cutters aren't trying to kill themselves, so there's no reason for the injuries to be severe. While some cutters do want people to notice and care, most self-injurers make great efforts to hide their wounds.

- **They're dangerous.** It might seem normal at first to be scared of a friend who cuts herself. But doctors agree that unless the self-injury is because of some type of rare psychosis, the cutter is not a danger to anyone else. Still, self-injurers run the risk of being rejected, made fun of, and even kicked out of school if they're caught hurting themselves—which only makes them feel like more of an outcast . . . which leads to more cutting.

- **They have Munchausen's.** Some people assume that self-injurers are the same as people with Munchausen's syndrome, an illness in which people purposely hurt themselves so that they can get medical attention. In fact, people who self-injure do it in secret, and their goal is the actual injury, as opposed to the treatment, which is why Munchausen's patients injure themselves.

Who's Doing This?

They must be the weirdos, right? The sad, mopey, uncool freaks. Not true. Famous people who have reportedly admitted to self-cutting include Johnny Depp, Christina Ricci, Shirley Manson, Courtney Love, and Fiona Apple. Even Princess Diana used to hurt herself.

The typical self-injurer in America today is a teenage girl, middle or upper class, with medium to high intelligence and low self-esteem. She's more likely to be a perfectionist, a great athlete, an A student, a "good girl," than a loser. Some of those girls may even come from what looks like a perfect family, but it could be a family where everyone's outer smiles are more important than actually talking about what's really happening on the inside. And she's probably suffering from some other sort of emotional problem, like the ones described later in this chapter.

"The first time someone self-injures is usually when puberty hits," says Karen Conterio, administrative director of Self-Abuse Finally Ends Alternatives (S.A.F.E. Alternatives), a sixteen-year-old program dedicated to stopping self-injury. "Teens by nature are pretty volatile, and when something major happens, they're just devastated." That means that a breakup, a rejection, or a fight that an older person wouldn't even be fazed by may overwhelm someone who's never been through it. "They usually pick something up and impulsively scratch," says Conterio, "and then they feel a sense of relief, and it starts to be something regular. It's not that much different from biting your nails, except it's less socially acceptable and physically more dangerous." And if a girl does carve a word in her arm, it's more likely to be something like "ugly" or "fat" than her boyfriend's name.

As with suicide, gay and lesbian teens tend to self-injure at a rate higher than other kids. "It's hard enough to talk to your parents when you're a teen," says Conterio. "Kids who are gay feel even more set apart from both their families and other people, and the cycles of self-abuse are more likely to start." As you may know, part of what can make teenagers miserable is feeling different, or like no one understands them. Gay teens who feel they can't tell anyone they're gay are at particularly high risk of becoming cutters.

Sasha, 23 · Fort Wayne, IN

Sasha (the same one mentioned earlier in this chapter) isn't a teenager anymore, but she tells her story about cutting to whoever will listen. She wants to get the word out that you can get help. She's pretty shy—she says she has to leave when she finds herself in big groups because she gets so anxious, but her best friends understand her and try to help her feel more comfortable in any situation.

I always thought I had a really cool family, and I always thought that we were pretty healthy. But we weren't. When I was little, my dad drank. I have two sisters, and we all think there was an incident of abuse with him, just one thing that happened to me, but it took me a long time to remember that.

I've always known I was different than other kids. I've been diagnosed with attention deficit disorder and obsessive-compulsive disorder. I was held back in third grade. I always acted like I was happy, but inside I was more and more sad. In middle school, that's when people really started picking on me, tripping me in the halls and things like that.

I did it a couple of times throughout high school, but I knew my parents would figure it out, so I didn't do it that much. I punched walls, though—I'd always done that—so hard I'd hurt my hands. When I went to college, I was ten hours from my home and everything that I knew. I didn't know anyone. That first semester, everything just kind of fell apart. I started cutting every week, mostly on my shoulders and arms. I'd do it for a while, then quit. Then my friends would start to notice. They made me go to counseling, but then I'd go home for a vacation or something and it would start up again.

My junior year, my roommate and I were best friends. She'd met me after I quit cutting for a while, but we had a really unhealthy relationship. We were too close, we'd stay up all night talking, we pushed our beds together. We never did anything, but I was feeling attracted to her, and I didn't know how to deal with that. We were at a Christian college. I didn't understand those feelings. I felt like I was evil. I hadn't cut in over a year, and that was a big deal. Two days after my no-cutting anniversary, I did it again. I wanted to test my friend—I had to make sure she'd like me while I was cutting, not just since I was over it.

It made things bad between us, and after Christmas vacation that year, things just weren't the same. I cut my wrists so bad I had to get stitches. At the time, I told the doctor that I cut myself on a light bulb, which was true—I just didn't mention that I'd done it on purpose. They let me go, but a couple of days later I did the same thing to the other wrist. This time there was no faking it. My friends called my teacher's husband, who's a doctor. He said I had to go to the ER, and they said I'd have to be committed to the psych ward for at least three days.

That was the worst. I was out of control, and I hated that. They took away all my rights. I had to strip down and wear their stupid little gown. I had nothing in my room, they kept me up until four A.M. making me talk. They wouldn't tell my friends if I was okay, but they called my parents. They woke me up in the middle of the night and put some kind of thing on my head to measure my brain waves. After a few days, I found out I'd been kicked out of school for it. They thought I was bad for the other kids to be around, or that I was a danger. The next day, I went into the main room with all the other people in the ward, and that's when I really decided I wanted to change; I didn't even care how. Cutting used to make me feel in control—but now it had cost me everything.

I prayed a lot—that's a big part of who I am and how I've made it through. I know some people would disagree, and that's fine. But I think God put all the right people in place to help me. I went home with my parents after that and started seeing a counselor. After a semester off, I enrolled here. It's a big university, and my first semester I really didn't know anyone, so I just sat in my room. But this semester I've gotten into a Christian group, and that's really helped me meet people.

I've had a few backslides, and I think that's okay. I visited with my old roommate a couple of times and we were still pretty attached for a while. We finally started talking about the sexual attraction we'd never addressed. I finally thought I could be honest with her, and then she got a boyfriend. I pushed too hard, and she stopped talking to me.

I'm getting more comfortable here. I don't have a lot in common with most of the people, but I'm not as scared. One day, one of my roommates said that her ex-boyfriend was crazy and once cut himself. Before, that would have ruined everything, and I would have gone into a hole. But now I have a healthy relationship with who I am, and I was like, "You know what? I screwed up, I did that too." But it's not a big deal. And I see a counselor here regularly. Some of the transitions have been hard, but I finally found someone I could go to all the time to talk to.

A lot of people think self-injurers cut for attention. There probably are some people who do, but most of us hide it. I didn't want anyone to know I did it. I felt bad because it made my friends upset. I felt vulnerable when they knew. And it's wrong for cutters to think that it's enough to confide in another teenager. It's good to tell someone, but another kid is too young to handle it; you may hurt your friend more than you help yourself.

People don't understand that cutting does benefit us. It's awful, but it's not different from drinking or drugs or any other addiction. People do that, and they can't stop, and it's the same sort of self-medication. When you cut, there are chemicals that get released. I don't know the physiology of it, but I know that something real happens inside.

I was confused for a while, but now I know I can choose the right path for myself. I feel like I've changed. Even my friends who knew me a year ago, they look at me and say I'm a different person. I want to help other people who are different, to be involved in some sort of outreach.

It's not just girls who cut; there are guy cutters as well. "I've worked with many males who are also cutters and burners," says Larry Schor, Ph.D., coordinator of therapeutic services at the State University of West Georgia, who has been working as an adolescent therapist for more than ten years. The vast majority of cutters are female, however. "I wonder if this has something to do with social factors, which provide more acceptance of males expressing rage." When guys get mad, it's normal for them to blow up, curse, yell, or punch walls; in fact, many people think it just shows how manly they are. Girls who feel they aren't allowed to do such things are more likely to take out their rage on themselves, thinking there's something wrong with them for feeling that way.

"I know there are some guys who do it, but it's mostly girls," says a sixteen-year-old female self-injurer. "Nobody really respects girls, and we don't have any way to be seen except as sex objects. We're criticized because we don't look like a model or we aren't as skinny as someone else. Even though it's unpopular for a guy to talk about his feelings, if a girl gets pissed off she's being a bitch. They'll say she's being a Hillary Clinton. I don't even see why guys hate Hillary so much except that she's a smart, outspoken female. I can't even burp without my guy friends telling me I'm unladylike."

But these same stereotypes make it hard on guys who may be cutting or otherwise hurting themselves to speak up and get help—there's this wrong idea out there that a guy should be able to take physical and emotional pain. "I don't cut myself, but when I get really worked up, I do hit walls, poles, doors, etcetera," says a nineteen-year-old guy. "But the thing is, I don't realize that it will hurt until after I have fractured my hand. I also don't see it as any problem at all, though. I figure it's much better if I release my anger or frustration or stress on a wall rather than at another person, which is what inevitably would happen."

Self-injury isn't a disease—but it can be a side effect of a number of conditions. Often people who self-injure also have one of these disorders:

- *Post-traumatic stress disorder.* This condition follows a particularly horrible event, usually some sort of abuse (it's also common among war veterans). Sometimes, a person going through something awful will disassociate, or disconnect, as a means of escape. When they recall the event, or anything else stressful, they may automatically disassociate. Self-injury may help a person stop feeling so detached from reality and snap back to the moment.

- *Borderline personality disorder.* This is a condition that can cause people to change dramatically from day to day: One day they'll hate something; the next day they'll love it. Their moods change from hour to hour, and they have trouble seeing "the big picture." So if someone with BPD gets mad at a friend, she won't remember all the good times; she'll just rage against the friend as if she's a mortal enemy. BPD patients are also very sensitive and codependent, as they're afraid of being abandoned. Patients with BPD often self-injure as a way of dealing with their intense, uncontrollable emotions. Not only is this illness hard to understand, it's also hard to diagnose, though therapy can help.
- *Manic depression.* This is also known as bipolar disorder. Affected people feel extreme happiness followed by extreme depression. The unexpected lows can cause many to hurt themselves.
- *Eating disorders.* Experts believe that as many as two thirds of self-injurers also have an eating disorder. Many of the same feelings associated with eating disorders (not liking yourself, feeling out of control, wanting to affect your body) are present in self-injurers, which may explain the overlap.
- *Obsessive compulsive disorder.* OCD patients repeatedly do certain activities like checking a lock several times a night or washing their hands in a particular pattern. With severe OCD, some people can feel

compelled to repeat these behaviors up to hundreds of times a day. Self-injury (particularly hair-pulling) linked to a feeling of need or ritual may be a result of OCD.

- **Depression.** Feelings of hopelessness or worthlessness may drive a person to hurt himself or herself.
- **Substance abuse.** Taking drugs or drinking fills the same role as self-injuring for many people—it changes their mood without forcing them to deal with the underlying feelings. Many people who self-injure (and may suffer from one of the above conditions) also use drugs or alcohol.

Why Now?

Doctors disagree about whether more young people are cutting than ever or it's simply more publicized so more people are recognizing, labeling, and reporting the behavior. But even with public awareness increasing, there are frequent misunderstandings about self-injurers. "People think cutters are crazy," says Conterio. "These folks are intelligent and artistic, and they're just desperate. They'd have to be, given the state they're in emotionally." Almost all cutters have one thing in common: They feel incredible pressure in their lives; pressure to be perfect, to fit in, to have a great life, to go to a great school. It's a great time to be a teenager because there are so many amazing opportunities out there, but there are also way more pressures than ever before to not just succeed, but to be Something Great. It can feel impossible to live up to such expectations.

Ariel, 13 · Albany, NY

Ariel is a little girl with big dreams. Standing under five feet tall and weighing eighty-nine pounds, she's an avid gymnast, painter, and bookworm. She loves school and hopes to become an orthopedic doctor, marine biologist, astrophysicist, or NASA employee. But for now, getting through middle school is her biggest challenge.

I am depressed. I had several people in my family die when I was little, and I think that's one of the reasons I am depressed. I have manic depression and I am bipolar, but I have never told anyone. Well, I told a person who was my best friend once, but instead of helping me she shunned me and I never told anyone after that. I got terribly sad and tried to commit suicide, but it didn't work. I have tried to kill myself about twenty times, because I felt there was nothing left to live for, but then I realized there was something to live for.

When I was little, I always thought I was happy. I started gymnastics when I was three, and did that a lot, and I played with my friends. I was probably depressed my whole life, but because I did gymnastics so much, I didn't notice—I had something else to think about. I did a lot of sports—I also run, swim, play lacrosse, football, and soccer. I got hurt a lot.

My depression got bad in January of 2000, when I stopped doing gymnastics because of injuries. Soon after, I cut for the first time. I used my Swiss Army knife. At first I was scared and didn't know why I did it. But I kept doing it. I cut my arms, legs, anywhere.

I cut, scratch, and hit myself. Lately I have been cutting myself on my legs, because they bleed longer than my arms. My left leg, especially, it's all torn up and wrapped right now. I cut every day now, and pretty badly. Yesterday I went so deep I almost hit the bone in my shin. I didn't mean to go that deep.

I feel good while I cut, like I am in control. Afterward, I feel relaxed and happy. I love to watch the blood drip down. Then I bandage it up. The blood usually soaks through, so I use an Ace bandage too. It's made me want to be a doctor when I grow up, so I know how to wrap things up and treat injuries the right way.

My parents have noticed my cuts, but only the ones that aren't so bad and look like scrapes. They just think I scraped my legs outside. Sometimes they'll see one they don't recognize, so I make up an excuse. Luckily, they believe me. I don't want them to know.

Cutters are depressed, angry, and scared. They need something to take their mind off that, so they turn to pain. I feel sad, angry, and alone in my life. When I cut I feel better because I am not concentrating on my emotional pain, only my physical pain. I like physical pain. Right now I don't want to stop. I don't know what would help me, I really don't. You could talk to someone who wants to cut, but I don't want to be happy, I want to cut. After a while, there may be nothing you can do. Only they can save or help themselves.

People cut because they feel alone, scared, powerless, and

depressed, and these conditions (and states of mind) are all on the rise among teens as life gets ever more complicated for them and expectations rise higher and higher. In response to the question "Why do self-injurers hurt themselves?" here's what teenagers had to say:

Loneliness "I think they're thinking they don't have anyone in the world that cares for them," says a fourteen-year-old girl. "I think it's a silent plea for help—that if someone would just notice, it would show that someone cares."

Low Self-Esteem "I know many people who think they are worthless, including me at most times, but it's not the way to live your life," says a thirteen-year-old girl. "Those people are seeking to feel more loved, but they're doing it in the wrong way. Many carry the world on their backs, and it's not good for them."

Pent-Up Emotions "My friends tell me a lot about cutting, and I've read a lot on the topic," says a fourteen-year-old girl. "This is what I think goes on in the minds of those who are into self-mutilation: There is a pent-up emotion in their system. Anger, sadness, or maybe the feeling they are lacking feeling at all, causes people to go a little crazy. They find that the pain of cutting and burning themselves makes them relax, gets rid of the stress in the quickest and easiest way possible."

To Show Their Pain "My friend was a cutter," says a sixteen-year-old girl. "She used to scratch her skin with safety pins and other sharp objects. She used to do it to her arms and legs and stomach. She carved a guy's initials into her leg this one time. She always wears a lot of revealing clothing, and she never lied about the marks. She'd show people and tell everyone about it. Basically I think people do that sort of thing for attention, some sort of it, anyway. She goes to a therapist, and she's stopped cutting herself, but there must have been a lot of emotional stress going on in her life to make her do that. I think it's wrong when people say it's unnecessary. People will tell you not to cry, but crying and cutting are ways to release emotional stress—if you hold it all in, you might do something more drastic."

Depression "I don't understand why anyone would enjoy inflicting pain upon themselves, but some people do," says a sixteen-year-old girl. "One of my very good friends used to do that constantly because a group of people were really mean to her and made her feel like dirt and also because her mom can be abusive. Plus, she was always stuck taking care of her younger siblings all of the time like they were her kids. She's easily depressed, and she cut herself a lot. I think it's really sad when people feel they have no way to escape other than through pain or suicide."

To Numb Their Pain "My little sister used to make long, thin cuts on her arms with razor blades when she was around fifteen," says a nineteen-year-old boy. "She said that causing physical pain was the only way to drown out the emotional pain she was feeling. My parents and her had not been getting on very well at that time. She ended up taking some drug and she stopped cutting herself. When she looks back at it, she is ashamed and disgusted, but I can see how it would make sense to someone as out of it as she was back then."

To Punish Themselves "I think that perhaps they believe physical pain will mask some kind of emotional scar that they have," says an eighteen-year-old boy. "Or that they somehow deserve to be hurt because of something they've done or thought. Masochism certainly isn't a new thing— religious fanatics have been doing it for thousands of years as penitence for their sins. It could also be a way for them to feel in control of their bodies, like getting tattoos or body-piercing, or eating disorders like anorexia or bulimia."

What Are the Signs?

Sometimes you can tell someone is cutting because you can spot the injuries. But if a cutter is good at hiding scars, you may have to be a bit more of a detective to figure out what's going on.

"I know exactly how they feel because I used to be one of them," says an eighteen-year-old girl. "In my family it was not okay to cry, and I went through some very difficult times, particularly in the early years of high school. I never expressed any of my emotions, so they just kept on piling up, to a point where I couldn't take it anymore. When I cut myself, it felt like a release. It's like crying when you are sad, but this time my tears came from the cuts I inflicted upon myself." Many cutters echoed this idea of feeling isolated, alone, like they had no one to talk to. Besides being isolated, there are other hints that someone you know might be self-injuring:

- Having unexplained or repeated injuries, particularly in the same place
- Wearing long sleeves or pants in warm weather (to cover up scars from cutting)
- Being a perfectionist who's been going through hard times
- Talking about a "friend" who self-injures

Monika, 15 · Chicopee, MA

Monika goes to Chicopee High School, which she describes as a typical assortment of teens: "some wackos, some sweethearts, but overall it's great." She loves anything involving art, and also plays in the band. She calls herself a crazy girl, not quite "Abercrombie-and-Fitch kind of girl," not quite brain. She's still getting over a breakup from earlier this year. (Her boyfriend of a year told her he was grounded and couldn't hang out, but really he was hooking up with someone else.) But she says that drama was the least of her problems last year—she was watching a good friend of hers descend into serious self-injury.

My best friend is a cutter. She had always had depression; she got it from her mother. She had it all along but never really showed it until this year. She started off by holding on to her arm and scratching at her skin until it bled. Later on, she started bringing pins with her to school. She pricked herself with these pins. Once she told me she'd swallowed safety pins.

She tried to hurt herself a couple of times at school, and eventually the school suspended her for the rest of the year. She was admitted to a local hospital, then a boarding school. She now writes me e-mails telling me about how she has learned to love life, but I've heard that crap before. I think she just wants another chance at attention. And then she gets all pissy when I start getting frustrated. There were times when I wanted to take my own life because of her and all her bull.

At first, the things she did confused me. I thought she was playing around at times, or wanting more attention. Then things got a bit more intense, and I was getting extremely frustrated. I felt as though all she wanted was attention. I started to back off. She never stopped when I told her to anyway. Like, if she was doing her thing with a needle, I'd be afraid she'd try to poke me. Later on, she started hiding so that I wouldn't try stopping her.

When I backed off and gave her some space, she figured I didn't care anymore. And when I did ask if she felt okay, she'd get pissed. It's really confusing and frustrating. Especially in the stage I am in now. Teenagers already have enough bull to deal with. School. Parents. All the other stuff. I have a lot of stress. My parents don't get along. My dad can be very abusive, physically. My grades sank that year. I almost had to stay back, but I got some help and managed to be promoted. The confusion got me very angry at many times. I just wanted to blow up in her face and tell her to get out of my life. But I know I couldn't do that to my own best friend.

I have a bit more peace of mind now. I don't have to worry about her blood on my books. I still try to keep my distance. In a way, I don't want to get too close to her until she changes, until she improves. She wants things to be the way they used to be. But she has to do her part. She has to realize what her life is worth. I'm ready to take her back at any time. I'm just waiting for her on this road that she has fallen back on. She can pick herself up. I've already tried.

I don't even know why these people would want to do that to themselves. I tried it once myself. I took a blade and cut my arm after my boyfriend had broken up with me, but I just did it out of boredom and curiosity. It amused me a little bit, how quickly it got swollen. But I realized I shouldn't do it over such a jerk. I could do better than him. And it hurt like a bitch too. I don't see why people say it drowns out their other pains. I guess my friend had her condition as an influence to her actions, her depression. I asked her many times, though, why she did this. She said she couldn't control her actions! This pissed me off. How could you not control it? How could you not control lifting up your arm and grabbing a blade? Why can't you just tell yourself not to? But that's her reasoning.

How Can We Stop It?

It can be hard to help someone who doesn't seem to want your help. "I dated a girl last year, and she would cut herself," says an eighteen-year-old guy. "She would find pretty much anything sharp and make little superficial cuts all over her forearms and wrists when she was stressed. Other times she said she'd just be sitting alone and space out and just kind of wake up and find herself bleeding. The pain would bring her back to reality. Part of it, I think, was an embodiment of the pain she was feeling emotionally. And on another level, it was a way to rebel against her parents, who hated it when she did that, obviously. But it was something they had no control over. One time she did it, and they committed her, and she went on antidepressants. As far as I know, she doesn't do it anymore. I wanted to help her, but I couldn't. From what I could tell, there was nothing I could have done to make her stop."

If you think that a friend of yours is hurting herself, the first thing you should do is talk to her. If you are worried that she may be in real danger, tell a school counselor or teacher. After that, the best thing you can do for her is to just be there. It's okay for you to tell your friend you don't want her to cut, but if you try to judge her, you'll only make her feel worse about herself, which could make her want to cut herself.

Instead, try telling your friend that she can call you whenever she feels like self-injuring and you'll just listen to how she's feeling. But if she starts being manipulative (calling you when she knows you're doing something else just so she can feel more important, or calling you after she's already hurt herself so you'll freak out), it's okay for you to draw boundaries and tell her you can't be her friend until she's stopped injuring herself.

"Over the last summer I was best friends with a girl,"

says a fourteen-year-old girl. "Her parents had a shaky relationship for a while and they like to blame her. Once she told me that while her parents were yelling the night before, she cut her wrist with a razor blade a few times. I told her to never do that again and that if she ever feels that depressed she should call me or write me a letter to express her feelings. That seemed to work for a while. A week ago she told me she couldn't find a razor and she actually started scraping her arm with a pair of scissors. I can't help but wonder how heavy the guilt would be if someday I couldn't stop her and she really hurt herself or even killed herself and I didn't even have a chance to talk her out of it."

If someone you know is self-injuring, even if she swears you to secrecy, you have to confide in an adult you trust. This is too big a problem for you to solve on your own, and you would feel terrible if she seriously injured herself (as some cutters do) and you were the only one who knew what was going on. If you don't want to feel like you're snitching on your friend, give her an option: She talks to an adult (offer to go with her if she wants), or you will.

It can be really hard to tell on someone who's cutting, and your friend may get angry at you instead of thanking you for trying to help. But it's a risk worth taking, because you may very well be the only person who knows what's going on with your friend. When cutters go on for a long time without intervention, they tend to make more and more severe cuts until, like Sasha, they end up in the hospital, or worse.

If you suspect a friend is cutting, who should you tell? It doesn't necessarily have to be that person's parents (if things were great with them, the person might not be cutting, after all) or a friend (the last thing you want to do is start rumors flying). Talk to an adult you can trust—a teacher, one of your parents, another older relative, or a coach.

Even when an adult is involved in helping your friend get professional help (since no matter what she says, it's almost impossible to quit cutting without help), it's important for you to learn more about self-injury so you can continue to be a supportive friend to her. Reading books or getting information from Web sites about self-injury might also give you a better idea of why she's doing this and how you can really help her out. And you should talk to a parent or counselor yourself, so that her self-injury doesn't do damage to you. It's possible for you to worry so much about her and get so wrapped up in helping her quit that you risk your own mental health.

"I had a friend once who was a cutter," says a seventeen-year-old girl. "I asked her how her arm got cut, and she said basically that sometimes she was worried that she couldn't feel anything at all, because nothing they said at school affected her. She thought that she was just an ice queen. So she cut herself, just so she would know that she could feel, after all. I knew she needed help, so I told my favorite teacher. A year or two later, the girl came up to me and said that she hated me for telling, but she loved me too, because now she was better."

Some people who self-injure benefit from specific treatments for their primary disorders (manic depression, eating disorders, and so on), and that stops the cutting. Sometimes prescription antidepressants and other drugs can help. There are also counselors and support groups that specialize in self-injurers.

There are currently two programs in the country run specifically to treat people who self-injure: One is run by Masters and Johnson at River Oaks Hospital in New Orleans, Louisiana. The other is the one that Karen Conterio founded, called S.A.F.E. Alternatives, near Chicago. The idea behind S.A.F.E. is that only the cutter can stop the behavior. They won't accept patients just because their parents or teachers want them to go: The cutters have to say they want to stop. Their thirty-day program includes group therapy, individual therapy, treatment for underlying issues, medical treatment, workshops on coping with emotions, impulse logs (diaries in which patients write when they want to injure), and a contract in which the patients agree not to cut the entire time they're at S.AF.E.

But it's not enough to get someone to stop cutting—the only way to end the cutting for good is to help the person realize why she's cutting in the first place. Is it to escape feelings of loneliness or despair or not fitting in? Whatever the reason, it has to be talked about so that the person knows there are other ways to deal with problems and emotional pain that don't involve self-injury. "Some self-injurers report failed attempts at therapy because therapists focus on the behavior rather than the underlying problems," says Larry Schor.

It's important to keep trying to find someone to help. If you are cutting and your first therapist doesn't know about self-injury, isn't willing to learn, or tries to diagnose you with something you know isn't your problem, it's okay to ask to see someone else. "I even have patients I treat over the phone, because there's just no one in their area who can help them," says Tracy Alderman. Cutting requires specialized treatment, and not all therapists will know how to deal with it effectively.

The Web is another great place to start looking for help (sites like www.safe-alternatives.com and www.self-injury.net feature medical facts and stories from teenagers). You can find out you're not alone, read other people's stories, and seek out a mental health professional in your area. But reading about other people who cut can be addictive, warns Conterio: "Many people get involved in these communities and it becomes their whole identity." They may make so many friends and get so absorbed that they don't want to get better, because their whole identity is formed around being a cutter.

For most people, self-injuring stops after five or ten years, simply because they develop other coping mechanisms and their life becomes more stable as they age. If you're cutting, that doesn't mean you have to wait to get help. Try taking notes on how you feel when you want to hurt yourself, and come up with

SCARY STATS

Some experts say as many as two million Americans self-injure. Results of a recent University of Missouri study showed the number may be closer to three million.

In one study by Karen Conterio, 97 percent of those who said they were self-injurers were female; other studies have found that between half and two thirds of self-injurers are female.

1-800-DONT-CUT, the help line for S.A.F.E. Alternatives, which offers information on self-injury and access to the program, gets over five thousand calls a month.

One survey of 245 college students found that 12 percent admitted to having deliberately harmed themselves.

BODILY HARM

> Fifty percent of self-injurers have survived some sort of physical or sexual abuse; 90 percent say they were discouraged from expressing their emotions; 50 to 66 percent have some sort of eating disorder.
>
> S.A.F.E. ALTERNATIVES

other ways to deal with your feelings. Working through these issues yourself is no substitute for professional care, but it is better than nothing. Ask your friends what they do when they're feeling that way. Your goal should be to substitute a healthy response to your feelings instead of self-injuring.

Bodily Harm: The Breakthrough Healing Program for Self-Injurers, coauthored by Karen Conterio, explains the entire S.A.F.E. Alternatives philosophy in terms that anyone can understand. It describes everything they do at the clinic, like the impulse logs and thinking exercises.

In the S.A.F.E. Alternatives program, patients learn to control their impulses to self-injure by understanding the feelings behind them. Through journal-keeping and lots of individual and group therapy, patients learn healthier ways to deal with their feelings and frustrations.

"Our first goal is to get the individual to recognize that they have a choice not to cut," says Conterio. "This can be stopped."

" Everyone else assumes that they know better than we teenagers do, and basically they make the rules without consulting those who will be affected by them. I guess it's also our fault in part, because we think that it's cool to be different and that we know better than everyone else—it's the 'you're always wrong' and 'I'm always right' thing.

We have this, I must cynically say, sorry situation—neither side will truly listen to the other. But that leaves most of us teenagers trying to find our way through life ourselves, 'cause we don't believe that adults are right in imposing rules that we don't see as logical and/or convenient. And we feel they're untrustworthy because of their seemingly relentless attempts to advise us, which most of us call tyrannical dictatorship.

Personally speaking, I see that the older generations have learned lessons about life, but then again, the younger people do happen to have ideas and suggestions, which could indeed be a new approach to things.

But the biggest gap that separates both these groups is probably the media. They make money by portraying teens as rebellious little twits who are the nuisance of society and must be stopped at all costs. You won't deny that these images make good media . . . and who's the media trying to sell those images with the advertisements attached to make money to? The older generations, who are the ones who generally regulate society. To some extent, miscommunication between the two groups is due to both sides.

Then again, the chances of this being read by anybody are nil, because no one would bother listening to any teenager. You get used to that after a while, because I'm usually seeing a bunch of adults who never answer why to things . . . but for anyone who reads this, thanks. At least someone out there is willing to listen, if for no other reason than to disagree."

—Benji, 15

Afterword

IT'S A SCARY TIME, BUT ALSO the most exciting time ever, to be a teenager. Every day there are new teenage millionaires, gold-medal-winning athletes, scholars, and heroines. At the same time, there are also growing numbers of teens who feel angry, disillusioned, and left behind. You probably feel sometimes like you have no say in what happens to you. (It's not like you would necessarily choose to take calculus, right?) And maybe you feel like no one listens to you. But please know that as teenagers, you have a very important place in this universe. Your behavior affects not only you and your family and friends but all of us, now and forever.

Connectedness was a theme that experts consulted for this book brought up over and over again. Feeling connected basically means feeling that you have a reason to care about what happens to the people around you, and in turn, you can expect that these people will care about you. This feeling of caring and interdependency is the ticket to cutting down on the chaos and, corny as this may sound, making our world a better place.

But how do you develop connectedness? Well, first of all, it's not only up to you: your parents, teachers, and other adults can help by being open-minded and non-judgmental, listening to you and making it easy for you to talk to them about difficult issues. But it's not up to them alone, either. You need to create a sense of connectedness not just for yourself, but for your whole community. How do you do that? It's not as global a task as it sounds.

It works like this: If you get even a bit part in a school play, you're going to get to know and care about at least twenty people, from the set designers to the chorus. That guy you thought was a drama geek might turn out to be an amazing juggler with a great sense of humor. That girl you thought was a snob could turn out to be a shy version of yourself. The more we all try to understand each other and see our similarities and celebrate (rather than make fun of) our differences, the less violence, teen pregnancy, and other sufferings of adolescence will plague us. Making an effort to know and understand what makes other people act the way they do builds connectedness.

Not that you signed up for this, but just by virtue of being a teenager, you have a major responsibility to look out for your friends (and even teenagers you know who aren't your friends). As you probably know, many teens in trouble will confide only in other teenagers. That means it's up to you to decide when you can handle a problem yourself and when you need to pull in an adult you trust to help you. Here's an easy test: What are the worst possible consequences of not telling? Could a friend die? Could someone (like a baby) be in serious danger if you keep quiet? Measure that against the worst possible consequences of telling. Yes, having a friend be furious at you or even dump you is horrible, but after speaking to hundreds of teens in this situation, I can tell you that your friends really will forgive you—no matter how angry they are at first. In fact, there's a good chance they'll even thank you (okay, maybe not right away, but eventually). Caring enough to help someone in trouble builds connectedness.

And give your parents a chance. Remember that no matter how much it may sometimes seem like they don't understand you, for the majority of you these are two people who you can *always* count on to love and care about you no matter what you do or say, and no matter how bad a situation you get yourself into. Before you think "Yeah, right" and blow that off, try it sometime: Get one of your parents alone when neither of you is stressed out or fighting, and really *talk*. If you want to bring up something that's difficult for you to talk about, start off by saying "This is really hard for me to say, but it's something I've been wanting your help with." Then go for it. Hard as it is to believe sometimes, your parents were teenagers once and they likely understand (or at least really want to understand) a lot more than you think. Communicating openly with your family builds connectedness.

And finally, the best thing you can do to build connectedness is what you do best: Take risks, and never give up. Stand up for someone who is getting picked on, bullied, or harassed. Try out for a team, even if it's filled with the kind of people you'd never usually hang out with. Try to figure out why someone is mad at you instead of just reacting to the anger. Give your mom a hug for no reason. Make today the day that you start thinking a little about getting connected. If you all think about it and work on it a little every day, you really can change the world.

Resources

Violence

The National School Safety Center
www.nssc1.org

The Grief Recovery Institute
818-907-9600—in the United States
519-622-7600—in Canada
www.grief-recovery.com

Teen Age Grief, Inc.
661-253-1932 voice mail
www.smartlink.net/~tag

Suicide

National Suicide Prevention HOTLINE
800-SUICIDE (800-784-2433)

Suicide Awareness Voices of Education (SAVE)
952-946-7998
www.save.org

The Yellow Ribbon Suicide Prevention Program
303-429-3530
www.yellowribbon.org

National Depressive and Manic-Depressive Association
800-826-3632
www.ndmda.org

Sexual Abuse

Rape, Abuse, and Incest National Network (RAINN)
800-656-HOPE (800-656-4673)
www.rainn.org

California Alliance for Statutory Rape Enforcement
www.wetip.com/wetip/sbstat/sbstagr.htm

Pregnancy

Planned Parenthood
800-230-PLAN (800-230-7526)
www.plannedparenthood.org
www.teenwire.com

Self-Injury

S.A.F.E. Alternatives
800-DONT-CUT (800-366-8288)
www.safe-alternatives.com or www.selfinjury.com

National Eating Disorders Association
(formerly Eating Disorders Awareness and Prevention, Inc.)
800-931-2237
www.edap.org

American Anorexia/Bulimia Association, Inc.
www.aabainc.org

Other Helpful Contacts

Child Help USA National Child Abuse Hotline
800-4-A-CHILD (800-422-4453)
www.childhelpusa.org

National Runaway Switchboard
800-621-4000
www.nrscrisisline.org

Covenant House Nineline
800-999-9999
www.covenanthouse.org

Parents, Families and Friends of Lesbians and Gays (PFLAG)
202-467-8180
www.pflag.org

Further Reading

Alderman, Tracy, Ph.D. *The Scarred Soul: Understanding & Ending Self-Inflicted Violence*. Oakland, Calif.: New Harbinger Publications, 1997.

Berman, Alan L., and Jobes, David A. *Adolescent Suicide: Assessment and Intervention*. Washington, D. C.: American Psychological Association, 1996.

Brown, Lyn Mikel. *Raising Their Voices: The Politics of Girls' Anger*. Cambridge, Mass.: Harvard University Press, 1998.

Conterio, Karen, and Lader, Wendy, Ph.D., with Bloom, Jennifer Kingson. *Bodily Harm: The Breakthrough Healing Program for Self-Injurers*. New York: Hyperion Books, 1999.

Fassler, David, M.D., and Dumas, Lynne S. *"Help Me, I'm Sad": Recognizing, Treating, and Preventing Childhood and Adolescent Depression*. New York: Penguin Books, 1998.

Garbarino, James. *Raising Children in a Socially Toxic Environment*. San Francisco: Jossey-Bass, 1999.

Gilligan, James, M.D. *Violence: Reflections on a National Epidemic*. New York: Vintage Books, 1997.

Hersch, Patricia. *A Tribe Apart: A Journey into the Heart of American Adolescence*. New York: Ballantine Books, 1999.

Lewis, Sydney. *"A Totally Alien Life Form"—Teenagers*. New York: New Press, 1997.

Males, Mike A. *Framing Youth: 10 Myths about the Next Generation*. Monroe, Maine: Common Courage Press, 1998.

————. *The Scapegoat Generation: America's War on Adolescents*. Monroe, Maine: Common Courage Press, 1996.

Pipher, Mary, Ph.D. *Reviving Ophelia: Saving the Selves of Adolescent Girls*. New York: Ballantine Books, 1995.

Rodin, Judith. *Body Traps: Breaking the Binds That Keep You from Feeling Good about Your Body*. New York: William Morrow, 1992.

Schneider, Barbara, and Stevenson, David. *The Ambitious Generation: America's Teenagers, Motivated but Directionless*. New Haven, Conn.: Yale University Press, 2000.

Schulman, Michael, Ph.D., and Mekler, Eva. *Bringing Up a Moral Child: A New Approach for Teaching Your Child to Be Kind, Just, and Responsible*. New York: Main Street Books, 1994.

Wolf, Naomi. *Promiscuities: The Secret Struggle for Womanhood*. New York: Random House, 1997.

Zerbe, Kathryn J., M.D. *The Body Betrayed: A Deeper Understanding of Women, Eating Disorders, and Treatment*. Carlsbad, Calif.: Gürze Books, 1995.